Memories
of
Watford

Part of the
Memories
series

Memories
of
Watford

*The Publishers would like to thank the following companies for supporting
the production of this book*

Main Sponsor

BRE

Geo Ausden Limited (Metal Recyclers)

Ballard & Longman

Brent Timber

Mapac Group Limited

Sindall & Baker Exhibitions Limited

Sovereign Brush Company Limited

Watford Launderers & Cleaners Limited

First published in Great Britain by True North Books Limited
Units 3 - 5 Heathfield Industrial Park
Elland West Yorkshire
HX5 9AE
Tel. 01422 377977
© Copyright: True North Books Limited 1999

ISBN 1 900463 24 5

Text, design and origination by True North Books Limited
Printed and bound by The Amadeus Press Limited

Memories are made of this

Memories. We all have them; some good, some bad, but our memories of the town we grew up in are usually tucked away in a very special place in our minds. The best are usually connected with our childhood and youth, when we longed to be grown up and paid no attention to adults who told us to enjoy being young, as these were the best years of our lives. We look back now and realise that they were right.

So many memories - perhaps of the war and rationing, perhaps of parades, celebrations and royal visits. And so many changes; one-way traffic systems and pedestrianisation. New trends in shopping that led to the very first self-serve stores being opened.

Through the bad times and the good, however, Watford not only survived but prospered. We have only to look at the town as it is today, to see what progress has been realised and what achievements have been made over the last 50 years. Watford has a history to be proud of - but more importantly, a great future to look forward to, into the new millennium and beyond.

Contents

Around the town centre

The High Street buzzes with life in this early photograph, the wide pavements filled with bustling shoppers, the carriageway busy with cyclists and lined with parked sit-up-and-beg vehicles and bicycles standing at the kerb. Note the delivery bike in the right foreground of the picture; those were the days when you could order goods at virtually any store and expect to have them delivered to your door. Passers by are ignoring the parcel left in the basket by the rider of the bike, but back then people were on the whole more honest than today, when both parcel and bike might well disappear before its owner returned. The handsome clock on the far right hangs above James Walker's extensive premises, where signs advise potential customers that not only do they stock Rolex watches but they also offer a jewellery repair service at 'moderate charges'. Further along are a number of other familiar names, such as Burts, Dudley's fashions and W H Smith, who have had a presence in the town for many years.

A scene to bring back memories! Cawdell's was one of Watford's favourite department stores, and the sun blinds were down and the shoppers were out in full force when the camera recorded this view one sunny day back in October 1957. And how many of our readers remember the very draughty alley between Cawdells and the Midland Bank - uncom-fortable for traders on the nearby market stalls! A prominently placed sign informs us that Tuesdays, Fridays and Saturdays were market days in Watford. A sharp eye might spot the National and Provincial Bank in the distance; today, however, the clink of glasses and the buzz of conversation is more likely to be heard than the quiet rustle of banknotes being

counted; the old bank is now the Old Westminster Pub.
The High Street has long been famous for the number of
pubs along its length (there were more than 20 at the
time); on the corner of Market Street on the left is the
Rose & Crown Hotel - at one time a major coaching inn in
the town. Registered with both the AA and the RAC, the
Rose & Crown was demolished in 1968.

Events of the 1930s

HOT OFF THE PRESS
The years of the 1930s saw Adolf
Hitler's sickening anti-Jewish
campaign echoed in the streets
of Britain. On 19th October 1936
Oswald Mosley's 7,000-strong
British Union of Fascists clashed
head on with thousands of Jews
and Communists in London,
resulting in 80 people being
injured in the ensuing battle.
Mosley and his 'blackshirts' later
rampaged through the streets
beating up Jews and smashing
the windows of their businesses.

GETTING AROUND
At the beginning of the decade
many believed that the airship
was the transport of the future.
The R101 airship, however,
loaded with thousands of cubic
metres of hydrogen, crashed in
France on its maiden flight in
1930. Forty-eight passengers and
crew lost their lives. In 1937 the
Hindenburg burst into flames -
the entire disaster caught on
camera and described by a
distraught reporter. The days of
the airship were numbered.

SPORTING CHANCE
In 1939 British racing driver Sir
Malcolm Campbell hit the
headlines when he captured the
world's water-speed record for
the third time in 'Bluebird' - all
his cars were given the same
name. A racing driver who set
world speed records both on
land and on water, Sir Malcolm
established world land-speed
records no fewer than nine
times. His son Donald went on to
set further records, tragically
dying in 1967 when his
speedboat - also named
'Bluebird' - crashed.

The Essex Arms can be seen to the left of this early photograph. The Essex Arms was an important inn during the 19th century, though it was later demolished when Cawdells extended their premises. This marvellous old photograph of Cawdells in an earlier era shows us that the store was advertised as having the 'Best value in general and fancy drapery'. The picture is full of life and character as scores of people crowd the pavements outside the store and the pub.

Bottom: Well-known, yet unfamiliar, this view gives us a glimpse back through time to the way things were. The date was 24th May 1935, and a mere handful of cars intrude on the peace of The Parade; spot the lone police officer (or possibly AA man) supposedly directing traffic in the background...his services are obviously not needed!

The 'sit up and beg' shape and shiny black colour of the few cars in this shot bring back those early days of motoring, before traffic became frenetic in its intensity and people could still cross the roads in relative safety. The Pond itself has gone through many changes over the years; the well-loved stretch of water was largely free of plants when this view was captured in 1935, making it appear somehow *wetter* - if water can be said to be wetter than normal. The photograph pre-dates the Town Hall, which five years on would replace The Elms in this scene. Note the bicycle parked along the kerbside on the left, and the window cleaner's barrow and ladders on the right; those were, of course, the gentler days when you could park such property outside a shop or workplace and expect to find bike, barrow and ladders still there when you returned.

Right: Road works are in progress in the High Street...so what's new? A whole string of workers on the right are hard at work - cable-laying, perhaps? Their work would not be connected with the building of the 'new' Town Hall, as the building's foundation stone was laid two years after this picture was snapped on 20th November 1936. Flat caps were the hardest hats on site in this revealing photograph. 'No hat, no boots, no job' is the slogan that reflects today's emphasis on workers' safety, but 70 or so years ago employees undertook many dangerous jobs every day without gauntlets, safety glasses, hard hats, fluorescent jackets or protective clothing of any kind, and reflected very little on the risk factor. In fact, in some occupations it was regarded as being somewhat less than macho to wear protective gear!

Note the four-legged form of transport making its way towards us in the background, reminding us of the days when noise from the town's traffic involved only the rattle of wheels and the trotting of hooves, and the only traffic pollution could be put to good use on your roses.

Traffic was building up in Watford by the 1950s, and a variety of different vehicles are negotiating the roundabout at the junction of the High Street and Hempstead, Rickmansworth and St Albans Roads. Note the pedestrian crossing in the foreground; although Belisha beacons are in place at the crossing, zebra lines have not yet been introduced.

The photograph is dated November 1950, and two years on Bert Davis would open the Chef restaurant in the Tudor-style building opposite the Odeon. How many readers remember the happy times they and their friends spent at the Chef - proving Bert's claim that people could have a good time without alcohol? The popular pavement cafe and Continental patisserie rivalled anything Europe had to offer. Bert's services were in demand by more than the locals; police officers would drop in regularly for prisoners' meals when their cells were occupied! Good Samaritan Bert also came to the rescue of the WRVS 'meals on wheels' service when their premises were demolished; for two years the voluntary organisation used the ovens at the Chef to heat meals for the elderly. The Chef closed in 1983, and Yates' Wine Lodge today occupies the Chef Corner.

Below: This photograph of the High Street in 1921 serves to remind us of a less frantic and more genteel age. Ladies in pretty summery dresses and wide-brimmed hats meet at the Empress Tea Lounge for afternoon tea, mothers walk out with their perambulators, while a lone police officer has little in the way of shoplifters, joy riders or pickpockets to keep him occupied. The corner of Clarendon Road, on the left of the photograph was long known as 'Dudley's Corner'; the display in the shop window would appear to be of - to our eyes - somewhat less than alluring ladies' underwear. Even younger readers will recognise the distinctive building, which was once the premises of the Watford Conservative Club and still survives today as the Halifax Building Society. Clarendon Road itself did not exist until 1864, when it was cut through to give a quick access to the Junction Station. The road was naturally named for the Earl of Clarendon, though its elegant residences were demolished after the second world war and replaced with modern office blocks.

Right: 'Sale time at Cawdell's!' screams the poster that frames the clock; good marketing this, as the clock was a focal point in the High Street as people checked their watches. This, we are informed, is the last two days of the sale, though the shop windows are still crammed with goodies. The people of Watford, who love a bargain as much as the next person, would have been quick to take advantage of the reductions in the early days of the sale, though now the majority of them appear to be passing by on the opposite side of the street. We have no date for the photograph, though the sale coupled with the abundance of hats and overcoats indicates January as the likely month.

Though some of the women obviously favour a neat little hat, at least one of the ladies has opted to wear the very practical headscarf which was still highly popular at the time. A headscarf could be folded and put away in a pocket or handbag, literally for the proverbial rainy day. This lady was in good company - Her Majesty has long been a keen wearer of headscarves.

Both pictures: The gentlemen's hairdressing establishment on the left 'through the passage' would not be able to offer the men of Watford their short back and sides for very much longer, as these properties were earmarked for the attention of the bulldozer *(Above)*. The years that saw vast changes in men's hairstyles, from the familiar fringes made popular by the Beatles to the longer styles of the 1970s, were also to see the beginning of the transformation of Watford. A note at the foot of the original photograph bears a note that records the date - 13.7.36. - and informs us that this was 'the demolition of Mrs Wise's shop'. The information will no doubt strike a chord with some of our more mature readers, who may recall not only the shop but perhaps Mrs Wise herself. Further along on the left we can pick out in reverse the name 'Clements', and readers will remember shopping over many years in one of Watford's most famous department stores. And when the shopping was done, did you pop across to The Brass Lantern, on the opposite side of the road from Clements, for a quick coffee or afternoon tea *(left)*?

Right: Recognise this junction? If not, it is hardly surprising, as this view of the Rickmansworth/ Hempstead Road crossroads was captured back in 1936 before the roundabout was built. Note the sign in the background, which advertises empty plots for sale for the building of shops.

Traffic was increasing at the time, and an official, probably with the AA motoring organisation, is directing the flow of vehicles at what could at times be a very busy crossing. The police force, of course, eventually took over this duty, and there was a time when every major junction had its traffic 'bobby'. Point duty must have demanded a high concentration of manpower, however, and it was no doubt argued that instead of directing the town's traffic the police force would be better employed in concentrating their efforts on the fight against crime. So a few at a time they departed, leaving the motorist with a legacy of traffic lights to contend with at each junction.

Watford's first traffic lights were installed in 1933 not too far from this spot, at the junction of St Albans Road, Langley Road and Station Road. Traffic lights, while no doubt keeping the traffic flowing smoothly through the town centre (in theory at least), somehow lack the personal touch provided by the good old British bobby.

Below: The Pond in February 1939 appears less well-cared-for than usual, but then at the time the whole country was poised on the brink of war. Only the year before, Adolf Hitler had signed the Munich Agreement and Britain's Prime Minister, Neville Chamberlain, made the mistake of trusting him. Many, however, had no confidence in Hitler and did not believe Chamberlain's assurance of 'peace in our time'; they continued to prepare for a war that they still saw as inevitable. Local air raid precautions organisations were established in every district, air raid wardens were appointed and trained, and the mass manufacture of gas masks began. The Home Office prepared a booklet entitled 'The Protection of your Home against Air Raids' which was sent to every home in Britain. To many ordinary people, however, war seemed far away, no matter what the 'bush telegraph' was telling them. They went to work, played darts in the pub, spent enjoyable evenings at the Odeon, and generally lived life in the normal way. Seven months after this peaceful view was captured, Britain declared war on Nazi Germany.

gantly-named Edmund Fearnley Whittingstall acquired the Coachmakers Arms for Abbot's Langley Brewers back in 1854, and that its coachmaker landlord, George Homer Ware, kept the pub for many years. The Coachmaker's Arms underwent at least one major rebuilding programme in its long life.

Top: So much has vanished from this 1950s Market Place scene - including, thankfully, the odd bullock or two that escaped from the abbatoir around the corner from time to time! Other things were more sadly missed, such as the Spread Eagle, whose distinctive sign can be seen on the left. Not long after this photograph was taken, the Spread Eagle's wings were clipped by the red pen of the 1950s planning department, and the well-known watering-hole was demolished. The adjoining shop, occupied at one time by Boots the chemist, has also gone, as have the Rose & Crown Hotel, the well-loved store Cawdell's on the opposite side of the road, and so much more in the High Street. The Spread Eagle and the Rose & Crown were two of Watford's many pubs; at the turn of the 20th century there were an incredible 35 pubs in the High Street alone. By 1970 many had disappeared and there were only 30 in the entire town. A few of the old traditional pubs still survive, though today's trendy establishments are more likely to have names like the 'Rat and Parrot' or the 'Moon Under Water'.

Above: It was October 1957, and on the day the photographer captured this view the number of pedestrians still outnumbered traffic in the High Street. In the 1950s the majority of people still travelled by bus, and in fact the driver of this one (whose number we cannot read, though Omo washing powder is the product being advertised) is so confident that he appears to be hogging the road for himself. Apart from a car some distance behind the bus, the only other traffic in sight is a solitary motor cycle - whose rider would today be wearing a safety helmet. Readers will perhaps have a soft spot for the Coachmakers Arms, another of Watford's historic watering holes. The records tell us that the extrava-

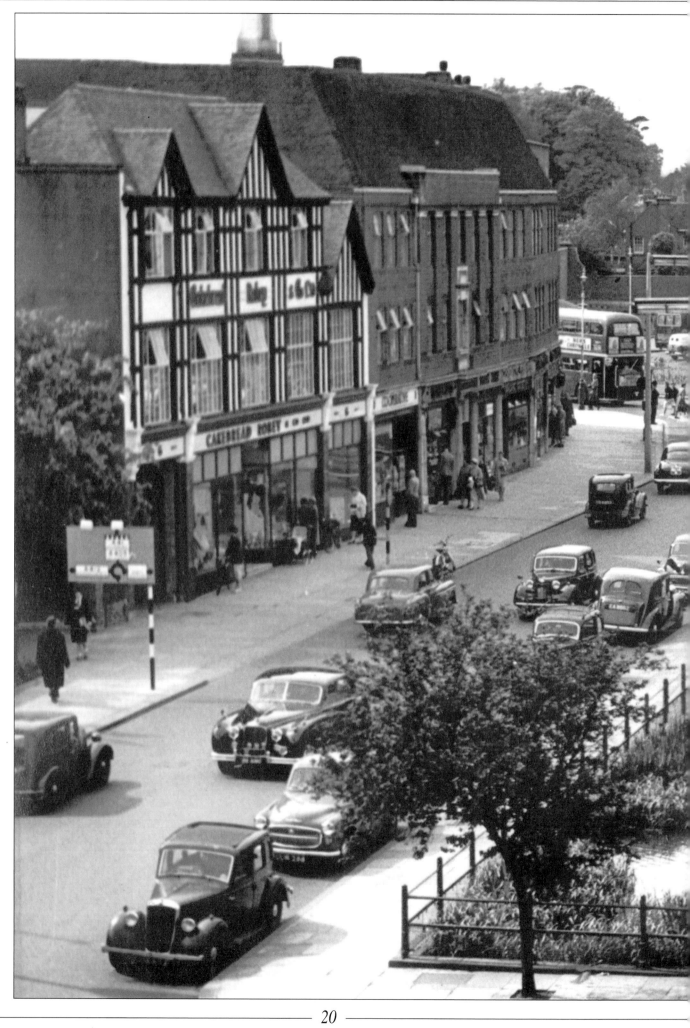

It was May 1956, and the cars that by this time were crowding into Watford High Street were beginning to change shape. Many older vehicles were, of course, still around, giving us the opportunity to compare the somewhat austere lines that were typical of earlier decades with the lighter, sleeker lines that developed in the post-war years, when colour was introduced into motor car design. Even towards the end of the 1940s the effects of the war were still being felt, and certain goods remained in short supply for some years. This included the motor car, as new cars were being exported as fast as they came off the production line.

Things were changing, however, and mudguards and running boards like those on the 'sit up and beg' design of the old-style Fords and Austins were set to become a thing of the past; headlights would be faired-in and incorporated into sleeker body lines, flashing indicators would replace the semaphore type (remember how easy it was to forget them and leave them sticking out?), and even quarter-light windows would gradually disappear from our cars.

'Premium Savings Bond Week' proclaims the banner that spans the High Street, and passers by with cash to spare, a desire to put some of it by for a rainy day and have a little flutter at the same time are being encouraged to 'buy some bonds'. Though we don't know the year, the banner tells us that the special 'week' was planned for the 17th to 24th March. How many of these busy shoppers - whose eyes are on the shop windows rather than the banner - went along and invested their money in premium bonds, which were a new idea at the time? The first premium bonds were introduced by the government on 1st June 1953, and the winning numbers

were chosen by computer, a real innovation at the time. Fondly known to all as ERNIE, the system (based in Lytham St Anne's in Lancashire) was officially named the Electronic Random Number Indicator. Over the years many premium bond holders have failed to claim their prize money, which today amounts to millions of unclaimed pounds. Time to dig out those old numbers, folks!

Events of the 1930s

SCIENCE AND DISCOVERY
By observing the heavens, astronomers had long believed that there in the constellation of Gemini lay a new planet, so far undiscovered. They began to search for the elusive planet, and a special astronomical camera was built for the purpose. The planet Pluto was discovered by amateur astronomer Clyde Tombaugh in 1930, less than a year later.

WHAT'S ON?
In this heyday of the cinema, horrified audiences were left gasping at the sight of Fay Wray in the clutches of the giant ape in the film 'King Kong', released in 1933. Very different but just as gripping was the gutsy 1939 American Civil War romance 'Gone with the Wind'. Gable's parting words, 'Frankly, my dear, I don't give a damn' went down in history. In 1936 - Britain set up the world's first television service - black and white, of course. The Queen's coronation in 1953, the first such ceremony to be televised, did much to popularise television.

ROYAL WATCH
The talking point of the early 1930s was the affair of the Prince of Wales, who later became King Edward VIII, and American divorcee Wallis Simpson. Faced with a choice, Edward gave up his throne for 'the woman I love' and spent the remainder of his life in exile. Many supported him, though they might not have been as keen to do so if they had been aware of his Nazi sympathies, kept strictly under wraps at the time.

Right: The red triangle on the sign on the far right informs us that this part of St Albans Road was an accident blackspot, which is hard to

Below: Remember Polyfoto? There's a name to take you back! How many readers still have a few sheets of those tiny photographs tucked away at the bottom

believe given the amount of traffic at the time of the photograph. Perhaps the lone cyclist will fall off his bike....

St Albans Road, traditionally an important route across south-west Hertfordshire, was also a pleasant shopping centre, and this 1950s photograph reminds us of the diversity of the shops in the area. Whether you wanted to buy a doormat or a bicycle, or have your shoes soled and heeled, this parade of shops was the place to go. Some traditional firms, such as Oakes chemist, whose premises are here occupied by Power Garden Tools, were long gone...when did they actually close? Many years ago, this was obviously the place to go, not only to have your films developed and your doctor's medicines dispensed but to buy the popular home remedies that had stood the test of time: castor oil, ipecacuanha, camphorated oil, Indian Brandee and Fennings fever powders.

of a drawer or in an old tin box? For those who are too young to remember, lots of very small pictures of your new baby or images of your child in his or her new school uniform were produced on one sheet, which could be cut up into single photos and popped in with Auntie's Christmas card or carried around in your purse or wallet. Polyfotos were immensely popular during the 1950s, though on October 1960, the date of this photograph, the shop was empty and was being offered either for sale or to rent.

Advertising lends its own kind of nostalgia to old photographs, and passers-by in the High Street are being advised to buy 'Golden brown Hovis'. Lovers of trivia will enjoy learning that the name Hovis (the winner of a competition to decide on a name for the bread) is a contraction of the Latin 'hominus vis' - 'the strength of man'. Hovis flour was first produced as long ago as 1885.

other paraphernalia of days gone by, pop into the hairdresser's for a cut and blow dry, buy half a pound of mint humbugs and a packet of cigarettes, purchase a set of jump leads for Dad's birthday - and still be home in time for tea.

Top: St Albans Road has seen many changes since this photograph was taken near the junction with Station Road back in 1959. The road was widened in 1961, and apart from a few of the buildings on the left most of these shops and residential streets were demolished. There were a fair number of passers by along the road at the time of the photograph; how many have noted that according to the large advert in the background, 'for fitness without fatness' they should drink Bovril?

Readers might like to know that Bovril was first sold as Johnston's Fluid Beef in 1874, and Bovril became the first client of an advertising agency set up by one of Johnston's employees. Within a few years his slogans, not without a touch of humour ('I hear they want more!' says one nervous bull to another), had made Bovril into a household name. The catch-phrase 'Bovril prevents that sinking feeling' was designed before World War I but was withheld at the time as a mark of respect for the families of those lost on the 'Titanic'.

Above: Don't you wish that today's traffic resembled this scene in St Albans Road? The view, with its three or four cars and a jay walker (who nevertheless appears to be in no imminent danger), was snapped some time in the late 1950s. Looking south from the railway bridge, we can immediately identify the buildings on the right (not an easy task in some parts of the town!). The names above the windows might have changed, but the terrace itself remains much the same. This little shopping centre still offers us a wide range of goods and services; today seekers after memorabilia can browse among a selection of clocks, china ornaments and all the

Left: A photographer dices with death to stop in the middle of the road while he sets up his camera to capture this view of a busy shopping day in the High Street. The traffic lights are obviously at red, and until they change to green the driver of the British Road Services vehicle on the right is obviously minding his own business. Would today's average driver react in the same way, we wonder?

In the background the names above the shops are those that have long been familiar to us: Saxone shoes - and in the distance, a huge but very old advert painted on the gable end reminds passers by to visit 'Freeman, Hardy and Willis for boots and shoes'; W H Smith, where you could buy not only books, newspapers and magazines but all your stationery requirements, and further along, Mac Fisheries, who still have a branch in just about every high street in the country. Mac Fisheries was established in 1921 as part of Lord Leverhulme's project to relieve the plight of poverty-stricken Scottish crofters by making them into fishermen. He ensured the success of the project by buying 300 shops as outlets for the fish they caught. One of the good guys.

Below: The shops in this rather nice old building on the corner of Clarendon Road (once the Watford Conservative Club) have had many different names above the windows over the years. At the time of this photograph they was occupied by the well-known tailor John Collier and Milletts, the workwear specialists. Milletts has long been a name to be reckoned with in the realm of workwear. Duffle coats, trousers, jackets, shirts, boots, you name it - if it was workwear - and you could almost certainly buy it at Milletts. Stuffed to bursting point with an immense range of goods, this store was the obvious port of call for any bloke who needed either working gear or casual clothes. Many of our readers will remember shopping at this branch of John Collier - and will perhaps recall (and be able to sing, though would rather not) their jolly little TV jingle informing viewers that John Colliers was 'the window to watch'! Gentlemen's outfitting has long been a trade to attract many rivals: Alkit (who specialised in cheaper clothing), Greenwoods, Hepworths, Hornes, Moss Bros, Austin Reed, and at the top end of the market, Hector Powe.

There was little traffic travelling along St Albans Road when this scene was recorded during the 1950s near the Harebreaks crossroads. Local residents are spoilt for choice among the shops on the right, especially those who were smokers. The advertising tells us that the nearer tobacconist is advertising Capstan, while the shop a few doors away is sporting a Players sign. Players have been pleasing smokers since

the enduring slogan 'Players Please' appeared back in the 1920s. Remember the rather romantic Players Navy Cut sailor on their early adverts? With 'Invincible' on his cap and a destroyer in the background, he smokes a contented pipe while reading his letter from home. It was 1971 before cigarette advertising and packets were required to carry a government health warning on the dangers of smoking.

Players have been pleasing smokers since the slogan 'Players Please' appeared in the 1920s

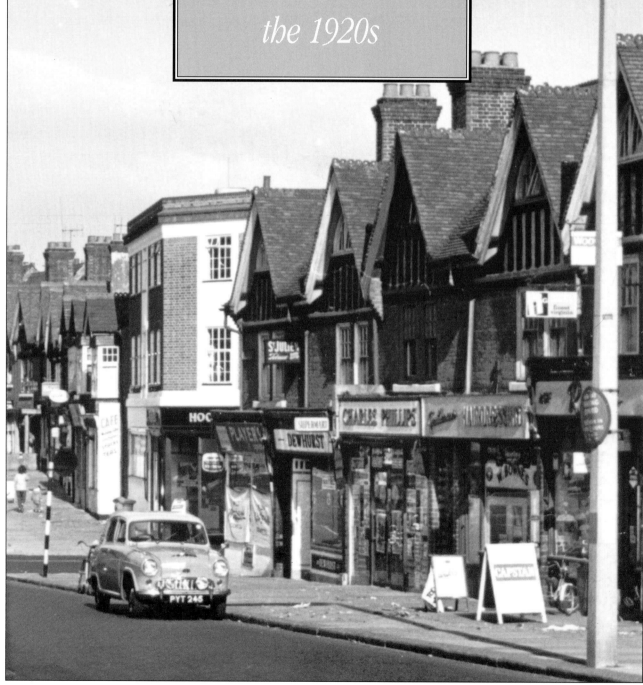

At leisure

Today's computer-crazy kids seem to have little time for the simpler pleasures of life - but these youngsters taking part in the Library Week at North Watford Library back in 1956 are obviously enjoying the children's quiz! Staff member Mrs Marjorie May was quiz mistress for the occasion, and her questions were the kind that the children could relate to. Perhaps some of our readers will be able to remember the occasion - and 40-plus years on will maybe recognise themselves as part of this little group!

The display of children's books in the bookcases illustrate just how much children's literature has changed over the intervening years. 'Never judge a book by its cover' is a well-known maxim that we all know; back in the 1950s you obviously couldn't, as they all look pretty much the same! Today's writers of children's books have more competition from computer games, football and television, and writers are finding that more than ever before they need to spin a yarn that grips a child's imagination from the very first sentence.

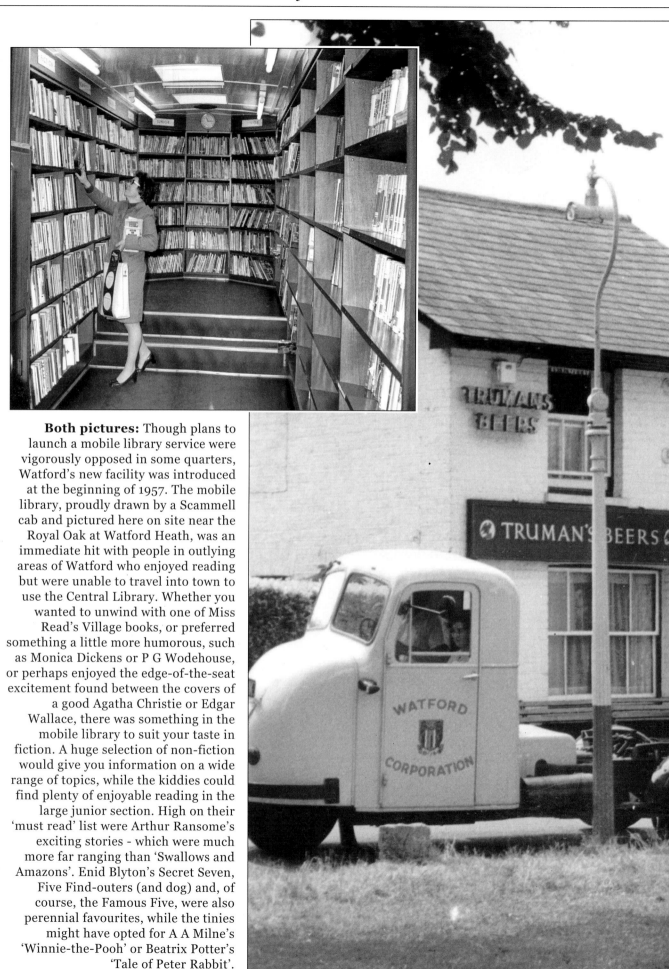

Both pictures: Though plans to launch a mobile library service were vigorously opposed in some quarters, Watford's new facility was introduced at the beginning of 1957. The mobile library, proudly drawn by a Scammell cab and pictured here on site near the Royal Oak at Watford Heath, was an immediate hit with people in outlying areas of Watford who enjoyed reading but were unable to travel into town to use the Central Library. Whether you wanted to unwind with one of Miss Read's Village books, or preferred something a little more humorous, such as Monica Dickens or P G Wodehouse, or perhaps enjoyed the edge-of-the-seat excitement found between the covers of a good Agatha Christie or Edgar Wallace, there was something in the mobile library to suit your taste in fiction. A huge selection of non-fiction would give you information on a wide range of topics, while the kiddies could find plenty of enjoyable reading in the large junior section. High on their 'must read' list were Arthur Ransome's exciting stories - which were much more far ranging than 'Swallows and Amazons'. Enid Blyton's Secret Seven, Five Find-outers (and dog) and, of course, the Famous Five, were also perennial favourites, while the tinies might have opted for A A Milne's 'Winnie-the-Pooh' or Beatrix Potter's 'Tale of Peter Rabbit'.

'Kiss Me Again', released in the US in 1925, was showing at the Central Hall when the photographer snapped this picture sometime in the 1920s. Marie Prevost, who starred in the film, is probably the alluring female on the advertising hoarding; Clara Bow, whose name we are more familiar with, also appeared, though not, we gather, in the lead. Daringly labelled as 'A sex masterpiece', 'Kiss Me Again' was a silent comedy in which a bored wife is tempted to stray (though naturally she remains faithful). The Central Hall opened in December 1913, with no less a personage on the guest list at the opening performance than the Earl of Clarendon himself. The 1,078-seat cinema also had the facilities to put on live stage performances (in case films - a very new development at the time - did not become a success); a seat in the balcony would set you back a whole shilling, though the less affluent could sit in the stalls for 3d. The Central Hall became the Regal in 1929 when the first talking picture, 'Sonny Boy', was shown. In 1956 came another change of name to the Essoldo.

Right: 'And in the Blue corner....' An appropriate setting for political sparring - though Sir Alec Douglas-Home would find little opposition at this particular meeting, held in the Town Hall. The Conservatives of Watford were out in full force to welcome the Prime Minister when he visited the town during the 1964 General Election campaign. He was in town to give his support to Frederick Farey-Jones, who had won the seat for the Conservatives back in 1955. Many Watfordonians were desperately hoping for that hat-trick, holding their breath as the election results were read out. They listened in suspense to the announcement: Miss M Neilson (Liberal), 5,797; F W Farey-Jones (Conservative), 18,744; R H Tuck (Labour), 20,224. With a majority of 1,480, Labour candidate Raphael Tuck had ousted his rival. Mr Tuck held the seat until 1979.

Sir Alec Douglas-Home, the 14th Earl of Home from 1951, had to renounce his peerage to become Prime Minister in 1963, but was created a life peer in 1974.

Below: The Oddfellows Hall in St Albans Road was for many years a popular venue for a wide range of activities, from concerts to serious meetings. By the 1960s it had gone 'eyes down' to bingo, a game believed by many at first to be one of those crazes that come along from time to time, enjoy immense popularity, then fade once more into obscurity. When this photograph was taken in 1968, the Central Bingo Club at the Oddfellows Hall was running sessions of bingo every night, proving exactly how many people loved to play the game. Listening carefully to the caller and marking off 'Kelly's eye' or those 'two little ducks'; the frustration of almost completing a line, only to be pipped at the post by another player; the tension of needing that final number 10, and waiting for those words, 'Wilson's den, Number 10' - and the final triumph of being able to shout 'House!' Over the years bingo proved to be no flash in the pan, and it remains popular today.

Cassiobury Park Arena was at one time a popular venue for many sporting activities; how many readers remember using their fine running track on their school sports days? Struggling to remain upright and on your feet in the sack race, or to keep a rather large egg from falling out of a spoon? Those were the days! This particular occasion (date unknown) appears to have been a gymkhana, or perhaps a local show, and various jumps have been erected around the arena. Did the event involve children, we wonder, trying the mettle of their ponies and displaying their riding

skills to their admiring mums and dads? The crowds were certainly out in full force that day, rooting for the horse or rider of their choice. More thrills were to come when the carriage racing started - a serious event that would have been followed with great excitement by the entire crowd.

Events of the 1940s

WHAT'S ON?

In wartime Britain few families were without a wireless set. It was the most popular form of entertainment, and programmes such as ITMA, Music While You Work and Workers' Playtime provided the people with an escape from the harsh realities of bombing raids and ration books. In 1946 the BBC introduced the Light Programme, the Home Service and the Third Programme, which gave audiences a wider choice of listening.

GETTING AROUND

October 1948 saw the production of Britain's first new car designs since before the war. The Morris Minor was destined for fame as one of the most popular family cars, while the four-wheel-drive Land Rover answered the need for a British-made off-road vehicle. The country was deeply in the red, however, because of overseas debts incurred during the war. The post-war export drive that followed meant that British drivers had a long wait for their own new car.

SPORTING CHANCE

American World Heavyweight Boxing Champion Joe Louis, who first took the title back in 1937, ruled the world of boxing during the 1930s and 40s, making a name for himself as unbeatable. Time after time he successfully defended his title against all comers, finally retiring in 1948 after fighting an amazing 25 title bouts throughout his boxing career. Louis died in 1981 at the age of 67.

Cricket balls, bouncing bombs and smoke alarms

It was only in 1997 that the Building Research Establishment (BRE) made the move from the public to the private sector. Now owned by the industry itself, it continues to have its main base in Garston, with a test facility at Cardington in Bedford and its Scottish Laboratory near Glasgow. Like any other company undergoing great change, there were opportunities but also uncertainties. However, the pluses have far outweighed the minuses. There is now a wider client base than was possible before. New contacts and partnerships with designers, engineers and other professionals have helped sharpen the skills and expertise of the scientists in meeting the needs of its traditional as well as future clients. Competition had never really been a factor before the privatisation. Now, deadlines and the need to win business for the company has led to a more flexible and multi-skilled approach. Even so, BRE continues to have similar goals to those that had served it well in the previous 75 years. Raising the quality and performance of buildings and improving safety and productivity in construction are still the overriding considerations. Recognised throughout the world for the quality and value of its research and advice, BRE looks forward to an even brighter and more exciting future for both itself and the industry.

It is perhaps hard to imagine that the home of BRE once resounded to the sound of leather on willow. In the 19th century 'flannelled fools' would be seen chasing the cricket ball across the field that was here. Spectators would picnic under the large cypress and cedar trees and batsmen would stroll around the boundary edge, handsome in their maroon caps and blazers. A cry of 'Howzat' and the umpire's raised finger would see one of them move off to the pavilion to strap on his pads, ready to face the demon bowler of the opposition. Those

Above left: *Sir Raymond Unwin, chairman of the Building Research Board.*
Below: *The Building Research Station at East Acton in 1925 - just before the move to Garston.*

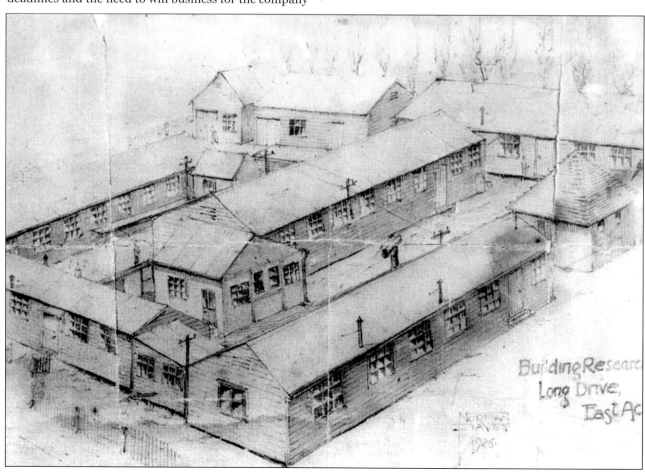

period of 14 years. The next owner was Robert Stainbank, a bachelor. This must have been a dramatic change for the servants and estate workers. Overnight, the house population had plummeted. Perhaps they thought they had gone deaf, so quiet did it seem! Charles Hegan, the next owner, was a keen cricket lover and member of the MCC. How he enjoyed the relaying of the cricket pitch and the installation of a new drainage system to help his beloved sport be played in tip-top conditions. His successor at Bucknalls, although more of a racegoer than cricketer, continued the tradition. To be good at cricket was almost a desired qualification to get a job on the estate. If you were a good gardener and could send down a fizzing googly, so much the better.

After World War I there was a real need to develop housing to replace the antiquated and insanitary homes that many people lived in. Few lived in buildings with bathrooms and central heating was a pie in the sky idea for the future. The millions of men who had gone off to the front had been promised homes fit for heroes on their return. It had been during this war that a commitment was made for central government to provide money for industrial research. In the early

days of ham salad teas and fresh lemonade were when the estate and house were called Bucknalls. The house, known locally as 'the mansion', was built on the 16 acre estate in 1855. It was home to Henry Creed, an army officer who saw long service in Afghanistan and India. On returning to England, he needed a large house for his family. His wife presented him with 10 children in a

Top: *Thirteen years after they completed the scale model 'dam', BRE employees Bill Newman and Norman Davey survey the model in 1954.*
Above left: *The model 'dam' can still be seen at Garston today.*

1920s the Department of Scientific and Industrial Research stated that it wanted to develop the knowledge of newer materials and the behaviour of buildings, conveying its findings to the industry and public. It also promised to deliver this in the sort of everyday language we would all understand. Sir Raymond Unwin, an architect, was the chairman of the Buildings Materials

Research Board, during the war years. Set up in 1921, the Building Research Station (BRS) had its origins in the Board's work and Sir Raymond's guiding touch. The first work of the BRS was carried out in temporary accommodation in East Acton. When the freehold of Bucknalls became available, it was bought by the Crown for £7,500. In 1924 the mansion and the 38 acres that the estate then included saw work begin on constructing permanent research facilities. This work, dedicated to the science of building, was the very first of its type anywhere in the world. The establishment opened its doors to over 40 staff the following year and work began in earnest. In those early days the Director had living quarters in a part of the mansion. The greenhouses were the first laboratories. The canteen and Geotechnics building appeared on the site of the old kitchen garden.

At this time the BRS was operating in what seemed like the heart of the country. It was only in the 1950s, with the coming of the motorway, that it could be described as life in the fast lane.

Around the time of the formation of BRS, the Forest Products Research Laboratory (FPRL) was set up. The Fire Research Station, that was founded after the second world war, would combine with the FPRL and BRS to form the Building Research Establishment in 1972. In those intervening years the BRS would start from a base of research into the effect of materials and weathering on the housing industry through to studies on a global scale. At the very beginning the ground rules were set. Research had to be methodical and scientific. It was recognised that it would be pointless to try to tackle problems without a greater knowledge of the principles of design and the physical and chemical make-up of the materials themselves. It was an era when there were no real scientific standards established

Above: *The R100 and R101 airships at Cardington in 1930. The right hand hangar is now a unique building research facility belonging to BRE.*
Below: *The senior members of the Architectural Physics Division in the 1950s.*

about the number of deaths that had been happening because of falls through roofs made of this material. New methods and designs in manufacture that would limit this problem would be the result of BRS testing and research. Study into the use of traditional building materials such as cob and thatch occupied part of the early work. Running alongside this was more experimental work into such as seeking substitutes for timber and alternatives for walling materials. The 1930s saw bigger and bolder strides being taken. Different types of cements for varying purposes, lime and plaster to replace the old slaked lime and the recycling of industrial waste such as clinker and furnace slag all came under the microscope of the BRS. Its work helped a mini revolution in the building industry. Thanks to the recommendations of the scientists, the use of soluble salts in rendering was identified as a cause for its failure. Plasterboard was developed to replace the old plaster and lath. In 1933 the 'brick cemetery' was set up at Garston. Its function was to test the durability of bricks under the conditions of natural exposure to the elements. The results of the study helped builders develop good practices in damp proof coursing and in the selection of the most appropriate materials for different climates and prevailing conditions. When war broke out again in 1939, half of the scientific staff were called up. Extra staff were then

for construction materials. The BRS took this on board and criteria and approaches were rationalised. Amongst the first matters to be examined was the place of asbestos-cement sheeting. There was a lot of concern

Above and top: *BRE's building research and test facility at Cardington.*

brought in as replacements with a special eye on the war effort. One major study was to have great effect on a particularly thrilling RAF operation, as well as the movie industry. BRS was studying the construction of concrete reservoirs for oil storage and the effect of explosives on reinforced concrete. It was given the task of building a model of the Mohne dam in Germany. The model was painstakingly built and experiments were conducted with a 2 oz gelignite charge fired three feet from the dam. The research results gave Barnes Wallis and his bouncing bombs the information they needed to send the Dambusters on their way into history as 617 Squadron, when it breached the dams in the Ruhr valley.

Since those days of early experimentation, BRS (from 1972 BRE) has covered an ever widening vista of topics. Heating and energy efficiency has come to the fore as we all become more environmentally conscious. Better

insulation for housing, air quality in buildings and the cause and effect of legionnaires' disease have been just a few of the case studies at BRE. Acoustics, drainage, refuse storage and artificial light flicker have all been under consideration. Major research has been conducted into industrial and toxic hazards, the ignition, growth and spread of fire and the benefits of smoke alarms and sprinkler systems. Structural tests on buildings, reports on disasters like the 1988 Piper Alpha oil rig, the use of fungicides and noise pollution all come within the scope of BRE. As it makes its way in the commercial world, it will continue to provide advice and recommendations that will help us all sleep more easily in our beds. Anyway, the comfort of the mattresses was reported on by BRE, was it not?

Above: *BRE's Environmental Building.*

Events & occasions

The flags were flying high around the town when Watford achieved Borough status on 18th October 1922, and people were out in full force to watch the ceremony. The Charter itself was brought down by road from London, and this photograph captures the historic moment of the Presentation of the Charter to Lord Clarendon, carried out at the corner of Haydon Road, the boundary of Watford Borough; the ceremony of proclamation of the Charter was performed in the Market Place. Luncheon followed the ceremony, and everybody who was anybody was on the official guest list, including members of the County Council and representatives of the three other Hertfordshire Boroughs, Hemel Hempstead, Bushey and Rickmansworth. Everybody loves a parade, and no fewer than six thousand school children were let loose to enjoy the razzmatazz of the great occasion, which meant an exciting procession through the streets of the town and in the evening, a fireworks party to delight not only the kiddies but their parents too.

The year is 1919, and those who worked together during World War I gather in the Drill Hall to remember the men and women who lost their lives serving King and Country. Beneath the banner that poignantly read 'Lest we Forget - Comrades of the War', a group of special constables and their comrades stand to attention on what is surely Armistice Day *(below, main picture)*.

The Great War was still fresh in the minds of Watfordians, many of whom had lost more than one family member on the field of battle. A mere twelve months ago in a railway carriage in France, Germany had surrendered to the Allies, the Kaiser had abdicated and fled into exile in Holland, and the four-year war had officially ended at the 11th hour of the 11th day of the 11th month. Every year thereafter, a two-minutes' silence was observed at 11am on November 11th out of respect for those whose lives were prematurely ended by the conflict; across the country an appalling total of 8.5 million people were killed in the Great War. The annual two-minutes' silence became a tradition, and throughout the UK everyday life came to a standstill as people stood respectfully in the street and traffic came to a halt. In what was almost certainly a later occasion, the moment was no less solemn as comrades-in-arms - women as well as men - met to remember once again those who made the supreme sacrifice *(right and below inset)*. In July 1928, the Earl of Clarendon unveiled the beautiful memorial statue 'Spirit of War' which stood outside the Peace Memorial Hospital. Mary Pownall Bromet's figures represented mourning for those lost in action, the many wounded, and in the centre, victory.

At the time, the years 1914 to 1918 stood alone on the plinth below the figures. We now know that the Great War did not turn out to be 'the war that ended all wars'; the future held yet more suffering and loss for the people of Watford, and the dates 1939 to 1945 were later added to the memorial with the legend 'And in remembrance of all other citizens of this Borough both military and civilian who have given their lives in the service of humanity.' The statue was later moved to its present site near the Town Hall.

What a marvellous demonstration of the Scammell Pioneer - though readers with that kind of sense of humour would no doubt be quick to tell us that it's enough to drive them up the wall.... The gentleman proving the truth of Scammell's advert 'There's a Scammell for every type of load' is Mr Pugh, who was the designer of the versatile Pioneer. What was Mr Pugh's position within the company? The year was 1929, and though photography was no longer in its infancy in the 1920s, few people owned a camera so the taking of a photograph was regarded as rather a special occasion. Proud of the company's achieve-

Events of the 1940s

HOT OFF THE PRESS
At the end of World War II in 1945 the Allies had their first sight of the unspeakable horrors of the Nazi extermination camps they had only heard of until then. In January, 4,000 emaciated prisoners more dead than alive were liberated by the Russians from Auschwitz in Poland, where three million people, most of them Jews, were murdered. The following year 23 prominent Nazis faced justice at Nuremberg; 12 of them were sentenced to death for crimes against humanity.

THE WORLD AT LARGE
The desert area of Alamogordo in New Mexico was the scene of the first atomic bomb detonation on July 16, 1945. With an explosive power equal to more than 15,000 tons of TNT, the flash could be seen 180 miles away. President Truman judged that the bomb could secure victory over Japan with far less loss of US lives than a conventional invasion, and on 6th August the first of the new weapons was dropped on Hiroshima. Around 80,000 people died.

ROYAL WATCH
By the end of World War II, the 19-year-old Princess Elizabeth and her distant cousin Lieutenant Philip Mountbatten RN were already in love. The King and Queen approved of Elizabeth's choice of husband, though they realised that she was rather young and had not mixed with many other young men. The engagement announcement was postponed until the Princess had spent four months on tour in Africa. The couple's wedding on 20th November 1947 was a glittering occasion - the first royal pageantry since before the war.

ments, other company workers (the boss in his bowler hat) pose for the photographer alongside the Pioneer as its ability to climb to an amazing height of seven feet is recorded for posterity. It is interesting to note that the measurement is marked in metres as well as in feet, though few ordinary mortals had any idea how much a metre measured.

Both pages: Links with twin town Mainz were well established by 1958, and children from schools around the German town were warmly welcomed when they visited Watford that year; the photographer captured their enthusiastic waves for posterity as they arrived at Watford Junction *(above)*. The Civil Defence Training Centre was the venue for a lot of the fun and games - and the presence of a number of members of the (considerably) older generation does not appear to have put a damper on the German youngsters' high spirits *(right)!* Civil Defence - part and parcel of World War II - was reorganised during the 1950s when the cold war was at its height, and the concensus of opinion was that preparation for nuclear attack was a real priority. Concerned council officials stressed the alarming fact that all the bombs that were dropped in Europe during the second world war were equivalent to a single H-bomb. As the years went by, however, and fears of nuclear attack receded, Britain's relations with what was then the USSR improved. In 1984 Novgorod, in north west Russia, became Watford's third twin town - and it gave the people of Watford a real thrill to establish firm links with Russia. The links with Novgorod - the largest of Watford's twin towns - were set up because Novgorod was already twinned with Nanterre, Watford's second twin town. Further exciting links were to follow, with the American town of Wilmington in 1985 and with Pesaro in Italy in 1988. The relationships that have been forged with so many different towns have over the years given Watfordians the opportunity to learn about (and in many cases experience for themselves) the rich culture to be found not only in Europe but in countries much further afield.

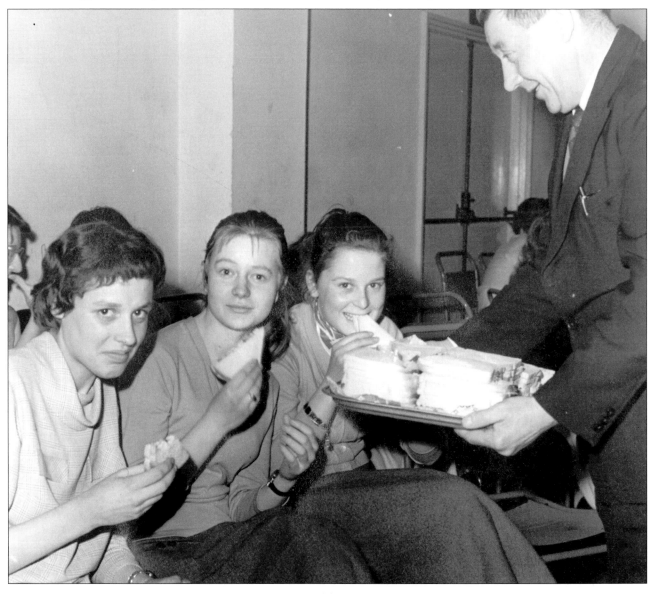

Events of the 1940s

MELODY MAKERS

The songs of radio personalities such as Bing Crosby and Vera Lynn were whistled, sung and hummed everywhere during the 1940s. The 'forces' sweetheart' brought hope to war-torn Britain with 'When the Lights go on Again', while the popular crooner's 'White Christmas' is still played around Christmas time even today. Who can forget songs like 'People Will Say we're in Love', 'Don't Fence Me In', 'Zip-a-dee-doo-dah', and 'Riders in the Sky'?

INVENTION AND TECHNOLOGY

Inspired by quick-drying printers' ink, in 1945 Hungarian journalist Laszlo Biro developed a ballpoint pen which released viscous ink from its own reservoir as the writer moved the pen across the page. An American inventor was working on a similar idea at the same time, but it was Biro's name that stuck. A few years later Baron Bich developed a low cost version of the pen, and the 'Bic' ballpoint went on sale in France in 1953.

SCIENCE AND DISCOVERY

In 1943 Ukrainian-born biochemist Selman Abraham Waksman made a significant discovery. While studying organisms found in soil he discovered an antibiotic (a name Waksman himself coined) which was later found to be the very first effective treatment for tuberculosis. A major killer for thousands of years, even the writings of the ancient Egyptians contain stories of people suffering from tuberculosis. Waksman's development of streptomycin brought him the 1952 Nobel Prize for Medicine.

Watford's politics have swung at regular intervals from Blue to Red and back again, and excitement was in the air back in 1959 when the Prime Minister, the Rt Hon Harold Macmillan, took up his stand behind the microphones to give his personal support to Frederick Farey-Jones, the Conservative

candidate for the Borough of Watford. This time, Mr Farey-Jones's opponents were Mrs R Short (Labour) and I S Steers (Liberal). Tension was high as the votes were counted, but in the event Mr Farey-Jones held the seat (which he had gained from John Freeman in 1955), with a majority of 2,901. Mr Macmillan himself remained Prime Minister until he resigned because of ill health in 1963; well-known for his work on improving Anglo-American relations after the Suez crisis, he tried unsuccessfully to obtain Britain's entry in the the EEC.

Both pictures: It was the 7th July 1936, and at exactly ten past five in the evening many of the Watford's offices and shops were closing for the evening *(above)*. But getting home on this particular day was proving to be rather more difficult than usual....

Roads awash with flood water was not a rare event in Watford, as the Colne burst its banks with annoying regularity after every cloudburst. This time, however, the heavens had really opened, and newspaper headlines dubbed the results the 'worst floods for 20 years' - though the memories of a number of local people actually doubled this figure to 40 years.

For the majority of people who depended on public transport, the outlook seemed bleak, as buses and coaches had been cancelled and the only way to get in and out of the town was by train. Meanwhile, the inside of the pavement, where the flood water was merely ankle-deep, appears to have been the least damp part of High Street to wait around for the water to subside a little. Unfortunately, many people would

find that shanks' pony was the only realistic means of travel. The lucky ones were those with wheels - either four or two; an oilskin-clad cyclist is making a brave though perhaps rather foolhardy attempt to negotiate the worst of the flooding, and we must hope that he encountered no hidden obstacles or potholes on his way home. But even when he eventually arrived at his own front door his troubles might not have been over, as in places the water stood five feet deep. Many marooned householders were rescued by boat, though even that mode of travel had its pitfalls; the bottom of one of the rescue boats was torn out by the tips of iron railings!

A few decades on, nothing had changed, and the driver of this Austin Cambridge (or Morris Oxford, which only had minor trim differences), is obviously finding it difficult to stick to his own side of the carriageway on the flooded road *(right)*. A large advertising hoarding in the background is encouraging people to buy the Daily Telegraph for news; tomorrow's news would no doubt be about flooding in the Watford area. So what's new?

Both pictures: *April 1947 saw people having to deal with the same old problem of serious flooding. Not to be beaten, however, the inventive residents of Walton Road made stepping stones from crates and boxes, and donning pixie-hoods and mackintoshes they bravely stepped out into the unknown (though one lucky lady has taken advantage of the offer of a piggy-back and is leaving the 'stepping into the unknown' to someone else!).*

And when the water at last drained away Watford's troubles, it seemed, were just beginning. Then began the mopping up operations. Incredibly, craters two feet deep and 20ft long were found to have opened up along the pavements, revealing fractured mains. And at home it was no better. Houses, shops and businesses were a sea of smelly mud that was messy to deal with and difficult to get rid of. Back in 1936 the weather had the last word, visiting the town a few days after the flooding with gales that tore down chimney stacks and fences and stripped the slates from roofs. Who said those were the good old days?

Drawn by the drama, a knot of people gather outside their homes to gaze in awe at the huge pall of black smoke that hung over Watford on the day that the British Moulded Hose works in Bushey Mill Lane caught fire. It was 21st June 1961 when smoke began to rise from the building from a small fire, which within a short time had turned into a huge blaze. The fire brigade was called, and before long an amazing total of 15 appliances were charging through the streets of Watford on their way to the burning factory. There were fortunately no casualties that day, though 70 fire fighters had a long battle to put out the flames. The billowing black smoke could be seen from a distance of 20 miles. When it was all over and the discussions began about the cause of the fire, a number of people put it down to the hot sun, though the assumption was not proved one way or the other.

Above: The people of Watford were out in full force to give a rousing welcome to the Queen Mother when she visited the town in July 1965. Looking as elegant as ever in her light, flowered coat and summery hat, the Queen Mother inspected the 1st Battalion of the Bedfordshire and Hertfordshire Regiment (TA) as they paraded in Cassiobury Park.

The people's welcome was a genuine one, as their affection for the Queen Mum has always been real and unaffected. It was during the second world war that people first began to know and value King George VI and Queen Elizabeth, and appreciate their many qualities. When the bombs started to fall, the King and Queen visited towns and cities across Britain, chatting with workers on the spot, and listening with genuine sympathy to those who had lost everything. The royal couple showed great courage by staying on in England when they and their daughters the Princesses Elizabeth and Margaret could have been evacuated to safety. They insisted that they be treated like everyone else, even to wartime rationing, and the King was almost relieved when Buckingham Palace was bombed. He felt that he could now identify with his people and look them in the face.

On the move

This page: The year was 1928, and the event being celebrated was Watford Shopping Week. Flags flutter gaily in the breeze from the buses that once ran between Watford Metropolitan Station (fondly known of course as 'The Met') and the town centre. The Metropolitan Station was the terminus of the LNER alternative line to London, opened in 1925, and no fewer than 70 trains a day ran to and from the City. Watford's problem was that the new station was some considerable distance from the town centre, and presented real difficulties for the elderly and disabled - and people in a hurry. The Met's answer was to offer a regular bus service between the station and St Mary's church, and four Albion four-cylinder single-deck buses were acquired and brought into service on 2nd November

1927. The buses, smart in their light brown and cream livery, varnished teak, and red grain leather seats, were a great success, though only a year later the service was taken over by the Lewis Omnibus Co Ltd.

their free time hanging around railway lines and stations - how many of our readers were among their number?

Whatever happened to this harmless hobby? The advent of television, video and computer games signalled the demise of many such innocent pastimes, and many of today's railway enthusiasts are in their fifties or sixties. Sadly, a small number of today's youngsters would be more interested in throwing bricks and stones from the bridge as a train passes, or in getting their 'fun' from putting obstacles on the line in an attempt to derail trains.

The nostalgia is all there in these old photographs - so important to everyone who remembers the age of the steam engine. But steam, as we know, was doomed, and the diesel and electric trains that were introduced across the country in the mid-1950s definitely lacked the character of the old steam engine. A wider view of the old Watford Junction Station will doubtless bring memories back to commuters who travelled to and from work every day *(top)*.

This page and overleaf: This was the first Precursor-type engine to be put into use at Watford, and the camera records for posterity the station master and railway workers, proud in their uniforms, and the bowler-hatted representatives from the National Union of Railwaymen *(above)*. And somewhere around would no doubt be a couple of train-spotting schoolboys, complete with pencil and notebook - part and parcel of every railway station; this occasion would certainly be one for the book. A few decades ago thousands of enthusiastic train-spotters, most of them boys, spent hours of

From previous page

We have no date for the photograph, though closer inspection shows us that the young woman leaving the station is trendily clad in mini skirt and knee length boots - those badges of the 1960s. Even without the clock the number of empty spaces in the car park would tell us that this is not the end of the working day, when wives drove in large numbers to the station to meet trains from the city. Younger readers will hardly recognise the view; the bus station has today taken the place of the buildings on

Events of the 1950s

WHAT'S ON?
Television hit Britain in a big way during the 1950s. Older readers will surely remember 'Double Your Money, Dixon of Dock Green and 'Dragnet' (whose characters' names were changed 'to protect the innocent'). Commercial television was introduced on 22nd September 1955, and Gibbs SR toothpaste were drawn out of the hat to become the first advert to be shown. Many believed adverts to be vulgar, however, and audiences were far less than had been hoped for.

GETTING AROUND
The year 1959 saw the development of the world's first practical air-cushion vehicle - better known to us as the hovercraft. The earliest model was only able to travel at slow speeds over very calm water and was unable to carry more than three passengers. The faster and smoother alternative to the sea ferry quickly caught on, and by the 1970s a 170-ton car-carrying hovercraft service had been introduced across the English Channel.

SPORTING CHANCE
The four-minute mile had remained the record since 1945, and had become regarded as virtually unbreakable. On 6th May 1954, however, Oxford University student Roger Bannister literally ran away with the record, accomplishing the seemingly impossible in three minutes 59.4 seconds. Bannister collapsed at the end of his last amazing lap, even temporarily losing his vision. By the end of the day, however, he had recovered sufficiently to celebrate his achievement in a London night club!

the right, and much of the open background has now been filled with modern office blocks. The new station with its up-to-the-minute facilities replaced the old one in 1985. The older aerial photograph shows us the station as it was in the early 1920s *(above)* when Watford Junction's extensive railway sidings on the LMS main line attracted industry to the town.

Letters of condolence were simply not enough

October 8th 1952 was a day of heartache and tragedy for many families who lost loved ones in this horrific train crash. Harrow and Wealdstone Station was the scene of the disaster, and the rescue workers and bystanders pictured here could at first only gaze in horror at the mangled wreckage and wonder just how anyone could have survived a crash of this magnitude - and how they were going to go about rescuing them from the wreckage of the three trains involved in the accident. The nightmare began when the Perth to London express, which had somehow got on the wrong line, collided with a stationary early morning commuter train. The London to Manchester express then cannoned into the wreckage of the other two trains, bringing down an overhead bridge. A heartbreaking total of 112 people were killed in the triple crash, and one of the most upsetting aspects was the high number of teenagers who died that day. Many of the victims lived in the Watford area.

The Mayor, Ald L C Johnson, decided that under the circumstances a letter of condolence was simply not enough, and within a day or so he had called on the families of all the victims in person to offer them not only his sympathy but the promise of any help they might need.

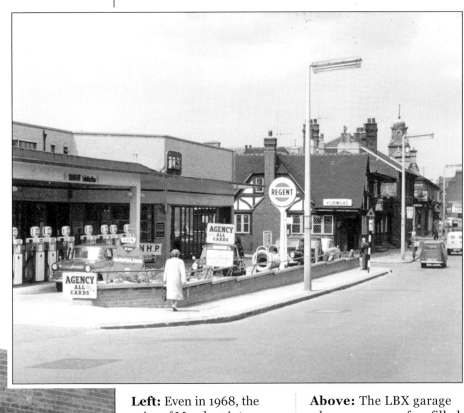

Left: Even in 1968, the price of Marsham's tyre bargains were an eye-opener at 20/-, which, for the benefit of readers born since decimalisation, was exactly £1! All makes of new and remould tyres - with an easy repayment service - were on offer alongside the cheapie tyres, however, as Marsham's was an 'approved Dunlop tyre service'.

At the time there was much public concern over various aspects of road safety, and when Barbara Castle brought in the first tyre law in the mid 1960s, specifying the minimum legal depth of tread which a tyre must have, sales in establishments such as Marsham's rocketed. The increased public awareness about the importance of driving on safe tyres led to a lot of changes in the industry. More tyre outlets opened, taking advantage of the growing market - and competition within the industry became more intense. At the same time the customer became much more demanding and discerning.

Above: The LBX garage where so many of us filled up with petrol in the 1960s was built in 1959 on the site of the Plaza cinema (which at one time had been the Coliseum). Those were the days when self service garages were unusual, so it is doubtful whether the LBX was self-serve at the time. More mature readers will remember with wistful nostalgia the time when you could drive your car into a petrol station and not only have the services of an attendant who filled up your tank, but who also cleaned your windscreen and asked if you were all right for oil. In 1960 petrol was four and sevenpence halfpenny a gallon (was the word 'litre' in the English dictionary at the time?), though a year later the price rose by a further threepence owing to an increase in purchase tax. In later years yet another motoring service took over the same site, and Central Tyres are today trading from this spot.

Left: This accident in Whippendell Road must have been pretty spectacular . What happened, we wonder, to cause this little car to end up on its roof - and was anyone hurt? And is the man talking to the police officer the driver of the vehicle? Perhaps not, as the overall he is wearing leads us more to conclude that he is an assistant at the little shop in the background, and could possibly be 'Uncle Bob' himself. Without knowing the precise date of the incident (which probably took place sometime during the 1940s), we can only speculate. The drama has naturally attracted a small crowd of onlookers, while the police officer has obviously had more than enough excitement for one day. Traffic accidents had become a problem even earlier than the 1940s; between the end of World War I and 1930 the number of cars on Britain's roads increased from around 200,000 to more than a million, in fact between the two world wars a staggering 120,000 people were killed in traffic accidents. In 1934 the Road Traffic Act introduced for the first time a speed limit of 30mph in built up areas, and made driving tests compulsory for new drivers.

Below: This photograph - taken in March 1949 - has a sense of briskness about it that tells us that these people are all going somewhere. Are they on their way to work, perhaps (after beginning the morning with Gillette?), or are they making their way home, tired and ready for a hot dinner, at the end of a long day in the office? Advertisers have found the railway bridge over Balmoral Road convenient for their posters, and while the bearded billy goat on the right advertising the advantages of Gillette razors is the kind of thing we would expect of the late 1940s, we might imagine that its counterpart on the left would raise a few eyebrows. After all, attitudes were very different back then. But even in the pre- permissive society days those who were 'in the know' enjoyed the naughty hint of suggestiveness in adverts such as this one, which encouraged people to avoid power cuts by keeping light switches in the 'off' position, while the suggestive implication would be lost on the more innocent (or ignorant?), who would simply take the slogan at face value.

Events of the 1950s

HOT OFF THE PRESS

The 1950s seemed to be the heyday of spies, and in 1951 the activities of Guy Burgess and Donald Maclean caused a sensation in the country. Both had occupied prominent positions in the Foreign Office, while Burgess had also been a member of MI-6. Recruited by the Russians while at Cambridge University in the 1930s, the traitors provided the Soviets with a huge amount of valuable information. They disappeared in 1951, surfacing in Moscow five years later.

THE WORLD AT LARGE

Plans to develop the economies of member states into one common market came to fruition on 1st January 1958, when the EEC came into operation. The original members were France, Belgium, Luxembourg, The Netherlands, Italy, and West Germany. The Community became highly successful, achieving increased trade and prosperity across Western Europe while at the same time alleviating fear of war which lingered on after the end of World War II. Britain became a member in 1973.

SCIENCE AND DISCOVERY

DNA (deoxyribonucleic acid) was first defined as long ago as 1953, and the effects have been far-reaching. The key discovery was developed over the following years and today DNA fingerprinting has become an accepted part of life. Genetic diseases such as hemophilia and cystic fibrosis have been identified. Criminals are continually detected and brought to justice. Biological drugs have been developed. More controversially, drought and disease-resistant plants have been engineered - and Dolly the sheep has been produced.

This long row of sleek and shining vehicles was on display in the Watford Motor Company's showrooms in the 1950s. Ten years or so after the end of World War II, post war prosperity was at last becoming a reality for many. Petrol rationing, which had been part and parcel of life in Britain since 1939, had ended in 1950 - and motorists were once

more free to drive as far and as often as they liked. The 1950s saw the development of important new car designs, which had a sleeker and more streamlined shape. For the first time designers were able to offer a wide choice of colours, and motorists who could afford to buy a new car were spoilt for choice. Here you could buy a new Sunbeam which, according to its description, was 'setting the pace in performance and leading the world in style', or if your taste ran in a different direction you could opt instead for the Humber Hawk, which was 'bred from success, born to lead'. All cars with real character.

This photograph of Tucker Bros garage in St Albans Road is one to bring the memories flooding back. How many readers can say 'I always used to fill up there'? Tucker Bros were much more than a National filling station, however; they offered a sales service as well as being registered repairers with both the RAC and the AA, specialising in

Austin, MG, Morris, Riley and Wolseley. Tuckers closed in the late 1960s.

And how many readers owned a Mini in the 60s? Thousands of motorists can identify the smashing little cars on the forecourt as their very first motor - and many are still cherished today by the affectionate owners who managed to

hang on to theirs. The Mini was introduced to British drivers in 1959 by Alexander Issigonis (who also developed the popular Morris Minor, interestingly the first all-British car to sell more than one million). The Mini's transverse engine made it possible to seat four passengers in comfort in spite of the car only being an incredible ten feet in length.

The little vehicle was practical, affordable and fuel-efficient - all features that helped to establish it as a firm favourite, especially with the student population and other hard-up younger drivers. Issigonis was knighted in 1969 for his contribution to British design, and by the time he died in 1988 more than five million Minis had been sold.

Birds eye view

> *With more than 2,000 seats, The Plaza was the largest cinema Watford ever had*

Many younger Watfordonians will remember the Odeon cinema in The Parade; the once well-loved cinema closed on 30th November 1963 and was demolished the following February. But how many readers remember the cinema when it was The Plaza? The Plaza was opened in April 1929 with the film 'Hot News' starring Bebe Daniels (who was better known as a radio personality than a film actress). With more than 2,000 seats, The Plaza was the largest cinema Watford ever had, and the building also boasted adequate provision for live shows, with an 18ft deep stage, dressing rooms and an orchestra pit. Back in the 1920s 'talkies' were the wonder technology of the day, and only three months after The Plaza opened, cinemagoers crowded into Watford's new Plaza to hear a singing and talking Al Jolson in 'The Singing Fool'. It was the first full-length talkie to be shown, and people came from far and wide to shed romantic tears over Jolson's rendering of 'Danny Boy', which became everyone's favourite song. The cinema was still The Plaza when this nostalgic view was captured in the early 1930s.

Events of the 1950s

MELODY MAKERS

Few teenage girls could resist the blatant sex-appeal of 'Elvis the Pelvis', though their parents were scandalised at the moody Presley's provocatively gyrating hips. The singer took America and Britain by storm with such hits as 'Jailhouse Rock', 'All Shook Up' and 'Blue Suede Shoes'. The rhythms of Bill Haley and his Comets, Buddy Holly, Chuck Berry, and Roy Orbison (who had a phenomenal three-octave voice) turned the 1950s into the Rock 'n' Roll years.

INVENTION AND TECHNOLOGY

Until the late 1950s you did not carry radios around with you. Radios were listened to at home, plugged into a mains socket in every average sitting room. Japan was in the forefront of electronic developments even then, and in 1957 the Japanese company Sony introduced the world's very first all-transistor radio - an item of new technology that was small enough to fit into your pocket. The major consumer product caught on fast - particularly with teenage listeners.

ROYAL WATCH

King George VI's health had been causing problems since 1948, when he developed thrombosis. In 1951 the King - always a heavy smoker - became ill again, and was eventually found to be suffering from lung cancer. His left lung was removed in September of 1951. In January 1952 he waved Princess Elizabeth and Prince Philip off on their tour of Africa; they were never to see him again. The King died on 5th February 1952.

The High Street bisects this eagle's eye view of Watford as it was in April 1932. Readers will immediately spot Cawdells towards the bottom of the photograph, with the Midland Bank nearby. These were the days, of course, when Charter Place was as yet undreamed of, and the old market stalls can be seen to the rear of Cawdells. To the left of the photograph, a sharp

eye will spot the Post Office, which was still under construction in Market Street at the time. This replaced the very small Post Office that had stood on the same spot. The adjoining public house on the corner is The Compasses, which at the time of the photograph had itself recently undergone major rebuilding work. As the

eye travels upwards the Town Hall roundabout, Upton Road leads off to the left, and The Pond just creeps into the top edge of the picture. The large square building on the far right is the Drill Hall, and many will remember the nearby factory with the chimney as Roger's Sawmills.

Ballards Buildings were overcrowded - at one time 39 of the 42 tiny houses were occupied by an incredible 226 people

More changes are afoot in Watford in this photograph, which dates from 1966. In answer to the urgent need of the mid 20th century - somewhere to park your car - the new multi-storey Car Park is under construction in Church Street. Church Car Park was built on the site of Ballards Buildings, a group of old properties dating from Victorian times when they were mainly occupied by railway workers and their families. Gradually, however, Ballards Buildings became overcrowded and unsavoury, and with the passage of time grew into a notorious slum. Thirty-nine of a total of 42 tiny houses were occupied - by an incredible 226 people. Also demolished in the same area were the slaughter-house, small shops and houses, a school and Watford's workhouse. Though a number of communities around Watford were demolished during the redevelopment scheme, many of these buildings in Market Street still survive; St Mary's church can be seen to the right of the photograph. The building of the Ring Road was soon to follow, neatly cutting Market Street into two halves.

The construction of the St Albans Road underpass began in 1972

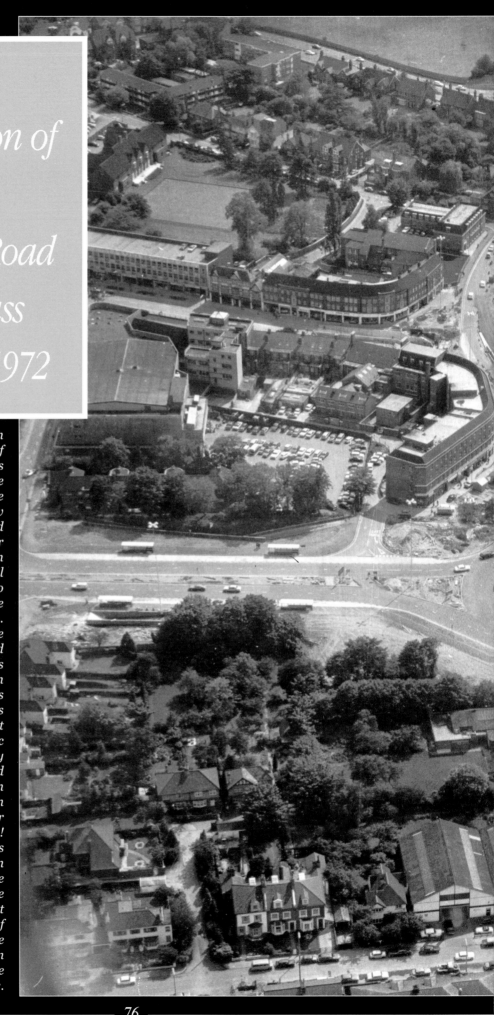

A scene of vast change in Watford as construction of the St Albans Road underpass got underway in 1972. In the years that followed the second world war few ordinary people could afford to buy a family car, and car ownership remained an unattainable dream until post-war prosperity began to become a reality in the mid 1950s.

The High Street formed the main route to Harrow and London, and traffic was becoming a real problem in the town centre; the bad news was that car ownership was set to double during the next 20 or so years. Traffic problems were not only Watford's; between 1953 and 1963 the number of cars in the country had risen from one car for every twenty-four people to one for every seven! In 1959 the M1 motorway was opened, and road building in and around Watford became a priority. Plans were presented in 1963, though it took a further five years of discussion before they were adopted and work began on the roads that were to change Watford for ever.

Shopping spree

Watford High Street was a very different place in 1925, and few readers will be able to identify with this unfamiliar view of the market place. At the time shopkeepers trading nearby had to put up with the livestock that paraded regularly past their doorways, which meant, of course, noise, smells - and the clear-up operations that were needed after the cattle, pigs and sheep had departed for the day. Nearby stall-holders too complained bitterly about their own working conditions which were at times made unbearable by driving rain, high winds, sleet and snow. They only had another three years to wait for a change, in the event, as September 1928 saw the opening of the new market. Stallholders were moved to Red Lion Yard while the livestock went to Market Street. Traders quickly found that conditions in the new market were still unsatisfactory - though they did appreciate the fact that electricity was laid on! In 1932 the market was covered over - and of course was eventually replaced by the up-to-date and comfortable Charter Place.

Wouldn't it be fascinating to be able to slip back in time and peep into Mandley & Sparrow's window, and compare the average house prices of 1957 with the cost of a similar property today? Though the estate agent only has half a dozen properties advertised in the window, housing was becoming more readily available.

During the 1920s and 1930s the lack of sufficient housing had become a real problem in most large towns and cities. Large numbers of young couples were having to live with in-laws, and many districts were overcrowded; though council housing presented a solution for the few lucky families, the waiting list was

Events of the 1960s

WHAT'S ON?
Television comedy came into its own in the 1960s, and many of the shows that were favourites then went on to become classics. 'On the Buses', 'Steptoe and Son', 'Till Death Us Do Part' and 'The Army Game' kept audiences laughing, while the incredible talents of Morecambe and Wise, the wit of Des O'Connor - often the butt of the duo's jokes - and the antics of Benny Hill established them for ever in the nation's affections.

GETTING AROUND
The 2nd March 1969 was a landmark in the history of aviation. The Anglo-French supersonic airliner Concorde took off for the first time from Toulouse in France. Concorde, which can cruise at almost twice the speed of sound, was designed to fly from London to New York in an incredible three hours twenty minutes. The event took place just weeks after the Boeing 747, which can carry 500 passengers to Concorde's modest 100, made its first flight.

SPORTING CHANCE
Wembley Stadium saw scenes of jubilation when on 30th July 1966 England beat West Germany 4-2 in the World Cup. The match, played in a mixture of sunshine and showers, had been a nailbiting experience for players and spectators alike from the very beginning when Germany scored only thirteen minutes into the game. It was Geoff Hurst's two dramatic goals scored in extra time that secured the victory and lifted the cup for England - at last.

very long. Though extensive slum clearance and house building schemes were devised, World War II interfered and brought many plans to a temporary halt. In Watford, the late 1950s saw the beginning of enormous changes as whole areas of old houses were earmarked for demolition in the town's ambitious road building and improvement schemes.

Bottom: Arthur East's was the kind of shop where you could not only buy most things you needed to take care of your pets, but your gardening supplies also. The signs in the window give us a fascinating glimpse back to the late 1950s (this photograph was taken in 1959). The store was an agent for Fisons, and had an awesome list of goods such as corn, seeds and manure for sale, reminding us strongly of Watford's agricultural past. But the small gardener was not forgotten, and your 'tulips from Amsterdam', golden yellow, crimson and any other colour you liked, could be purchased at Arthur East's. Surprisingly, according to one of the notices, the shop also stocked coal; most people had an open fire and few used any other kind of heating at the time. Nearby was the International Stores, where housewives stocked up on bacon, cheese, tea and other foodstuffs for many years. But this was the 1950s - a decade which saw the rise of the self service store. The trend started slowly, but it was the thin end of the wedge. Over the last forty or so years there has been a shift towards super- and hyper-markets and out of town shopping.

Right: How many readers remember buying records from W J Elliott's in the High Street? Elliott's was a high-class music shop that had been well known to the music lovers of Watford since the 1890s, when the firm still occupied their original premises in Queen's Road. In those pre-television years many people played the piano, and Elliott's extensive range of instruments was said to be the largest in the country.

W J Elliott's prominent advert for His Master's Voice records is one of the 20th Century's most well known trademarks; we even know the name of the little dog in the ad! The dog's name was Nipper, and before the well-known canine became famous his master, the English painter Francis Barraud, borrowed a gramophone with a large horn, simply because he fancied painting his dog alongside it. The Gramophone Company ended up buying the picture and eventually adopted it as their trademark. The company later became RCA Victor, and continued to use Nipper, who has ended up as possibly the most famous dog in the world. Elliott's, along with the other buildings in the photograph, was demolished in 1957.

of the Bristol & West has replaced True-Form. On the far right, across the road from the Westminster Bank (now Gap fashion shop), spot the Boots' building with its clock tower and dome. The original dome fell apart, though its replica now tops the tower of the Harlequin shopping centre.

Top: The SMC (Shirt Manufacturing Company) were having a sale at the time of this photograph. Many lines were being sold at half price at the well known firm; is this lady searching the shop window for a bargain, or seeing to her young family? Next door, Eastmans are advertising chickens at 13/-, while turkey was going for 7/6d lb. There was a time when small butchers such as Eastmans in the High Street were a common sight around Watford. Sadly, many of them are gone, together with the personal service we once took for granted. Small grocery chains and corner butchers were the traditional way to shop, and customers would queue to be served while the butcher cubed our stewing steak and cut our sausages from a long string hanging over the counter. A far cry from today's plastic packs! People might have had to wait a while longer to be served, but at least they had the benefit of personal attention from the staff. Things were to remain that way until the mid-1950s, when self-service shopping began to catch on.

Above: 'Expert shoemakers' would be a rare sign to see above a shoe shop today. Back in the 1950s, however, True-Form obviously were not only footwear retailers but also manufactured the products they sold. The building next door looks dreary and abandoned behind its boards and scaffolding. A number of businesses traded just here; how many readers remember shopping at Littlewoods Mail order stores, buying their cigarettes at Tucker's tobacconists - and popping into the Eight Bells pub for a quick pint? Littlewood's department store was eventually built here, later becoming Marks & Spencer; today, a branch

At work

The history of the Rose & Crown (sadly demolished in 1968) is exciting enough to fascinate anyone, even those who write off anything historical as 'boring'. For example, in the 1820s a large parcel was left at the pub to be delivered to London. Someone was obviously suspicious and opened the box; imagine his shock when he discovered the dead body of a girl inside it! The police were of course called, and some cunning detective work followed. In true Sherlock Holmes style the parcel with its gruesome contents was allowed to continue on its way - and the person who received it was arrested and jailed for body-snatching. The Rose & Crown's reputation, however, was already rather tarnished thanks to the shenanigans of John Greenway and his son, also John, who were landlords of the pub between 1770 and 1820. These two evidently led the keepers of law and order a merry dance; assaulting customers, threatening a tax collector with a knife - and allowing their pigs to roam the streets is just a small selection from the list of their misdeeds.

Events of the 1960s

HOT OFF THE PRESS

Barbed wire, concrete blocks and a wide no-man's-land divided East from West when a reinforced wall was built right across the city of Berlin in 1961. Many East Germans escaped to the West at the eleventh hour, taking with them only the possessions they could carry. The Berlin Wall divided the city - and hundreds of family members and friends - for 28 years until the collapse of Communist rule across Eastern Europe. Who can ever forget those scenes in 1989, when ordinary people themselves began to physically tear down the hated wall?

THE WORLD AT LARGE

'One giant leap for mankind' was taken on 20th July 1969, when Neil Armstrong made history as the first man to set foot on the moon. During the mission he and fellow-astronaut 'Buzz' Aldrin collected rock and soil samples, conducted scientific experiments - and had a lot of fun jumping around in the one-sixth gravity. Twenty-one hours and thirty-seven minutes after their landing they took off again in their lunar module 'Eagle' to rejoin Apollo II which was orbiting above them, proudly leaving the American flag on the Moon's surface.

ROYAL WATCH

Princess Margaret's announcement in 1960 that she was to wed photographer Antony Armstrong-Jones (later Lord Snowdon) brought sighs of relief from her immediate family. Just five years earlier the people of Britain had sympathised as the princess bowed to public and private pressure, ending her relationship with Peter Townsend, Prince Philip's former equerry. The Church (and the Queen, as its Head) frowned on the liaison as Townsend was divorced. Her marriage to Lord Snowdon itself ended in 1978.

(*Inset*) The Mayor of Watford, Alderman A Dillingham, is in full flow as he addresses the Borough Council, though the electric lighting - backed up by the clock on the wall - informs us that this is an evening session at the Town Hall. The Mayor, however, appears to have the full attention of all the members; what subject was under discussion that evening, we wonder? A well known figure in the town,

Alderman Dillingham was admitted Freeman of the Borough in July 1976.

The fine Town Hall and municipal offices is a building that Watford takes particular pride in *(main picture)*. Inflation makes us raise our eyebrows when we learn that the Town Hall was built at a cost of £186,000. The foundation stone was laid in May 1938, and the building was opened on 5th January 1940 by the Countess of Clarendon, who performed the ceremony in place of the Earl, who was unwell at the time and was unable to be there in person. The official opening of the impressive building was a grand occasion, and anybody who was anybody, not just in Watford but from other local authorities and neighbouring boroughs was on the guest list.

What were these workmen thinking as they systematically demolished the 19th century Cassiobury Park gates? They were there, we know, to do a job, but they surely must have watched the last moments of the elegant Tudor-style lodge and gates with a tinge of sadness. The demolition of what most of Watford regarded as a piece of their heritage came about so suddenly that it left most people stunned. As far as they knew, the demolition, carried out in 1970, was still at the planning stage, and decisions had yet to be made about resiting and rebuilding the lodge as a cafe. Behind the scenes, however, the widening of Rickmansworth Road was a priority, and Watford Borough Council had already made the decision to proceed with the demolition.

Were these two ladies chatting by the gates deploring their destruction as an act of Council vandalism, we wonder? The controversial action raised a storm of vain protest in the town. The rebuilding would have softened the blow, but it was judged that the work would have cost around £54,000 - a sum that the hard-pressed Council would have found hard to find. The lodge was never rebuilt.

Right: Genuine smiles are on the faces of guests and officials alike as Watford's first connections with twin town Mainz are set up. It was May 1956 when the cheerful group posed for this historic photograph - and it was just the start of the many good times to come. The German town of Mainz, with its history in both the printing and the brewing industry was an obvious choice as Watford's twin town. Mainz, situated south-west of Frankfurt on the banks of the Rhine, is well known for its successful wine industry. Johannes Gutenberg, who invented the first printing press with movable type, was Mainz's most famous son. Gutenberg's famous Bible can still be seen (though his financial partner Fust stole the great inventor's glory and in 1453 produced the first printed Bible under his own name). Ties with Mainz have strengthened over the years, and links with schools and other groups are now well established.

Below: The Pond has long been the pride of Watford, and in its long history it has gone through many changes. Unfortunately, we have no date for this photograph, and the style of dress and the vehicles in the background are all we have to go on. The 1930s would seem to fit the bill, and with picks and shovels at the ready, five men and their foreman use their concentrated muscle power in earth moving as they install a set of electrical illuminations in the pond. Were the lights installed to commemorate a particular event, for example, as part of Watford's celebrations for the coronation of King George VI in 1936? Perhaps some of our readers will remember these illuminations and their purpose - and be able to "shed some light" on the mystery, if readers will pardon the pun!

Below: Loaded with casks and barrels, and piled with crates of bottled beer, this lorry is ready to make yet another delivery to the many Benskins pubs around Watford. What a pity that neither the driver nor any of the staff were included in the photograph!

The history of Benskins' connection with Watford goes back more than 100 years. Joseph Benskin himself was just 13 years old when he got a job in the hotel trade and made a successful career in the business. In 1867 he moved to Watford and was able to buy Dysons Brewery (which was also known as Cannon Brewery). The young entrepreneur worked hard and over his lifetime he saw the company he had founded go from strength to strength. Joseph Benskin died in 1877. Further expansion followed, and in 1957 the company merged with Ind Coope; today they are part of Allied Breweries. Watford Museum now occupies the brewery offices, while the swimming pool was built on the site of Benskins works.

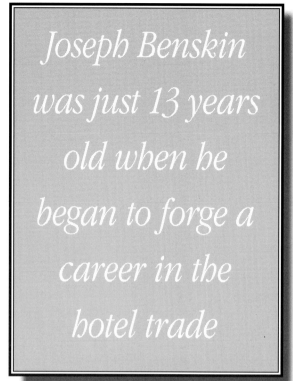

Joseph Benskin was just 13 years old when he began to forge a career in the hotel trade

Right: Before the advent of Play Station and Nintendo, children found escape from their humdrum school life in the pages of a comic - and many bought two or three different ones. Readers will have their own favourite; perhaps you found excitement in the adventures of the heroes in Victor and Hotspur (or Girl and Girl's Crystal). If your taste ran to humour rather than the edge-of-the-seat stuff you might have chosen the Beezer, the Dandy or the Beano. All favourites for many years. We have no date for this marvellous photograph, but everyone's favourite comic was on sale at the news stand on the corner of Market Street and High Street. Swift, Girl and Frogman were obviously favoured by the children of the day, while their parents were offered a selection of daily newspapers alongside a choice of magazines to suit every taste, including True Story, Picture Show and Daring Detectives.

Container and steel experts who began with a barrow

I wouldn't give you tuppence for your old watch chain, old iron, old iron. These words might just have been written for George Ausden Ltd. This company has been dealing in scrap iron and metals for about as long as the music hall song has been around. Although the company advertises in the local press and trade directories, as a long established firm much of the work comes to it through personal recommendation. Having been in their current premises on Lower High Street since 1928, it is not surprising that word of mouth has become one of the best adverts Ausden's can have. Everybody in Watford knows where to find them.

The company is very much a family set up. The three directors are the third and fourth generations of the Ausden line who have been involved. Grant and Steve Ausden are busy on the daily front of the business, but father John retired in 1995. As that was his 65th birthday, he had given it more than a good shot! In addition, cousin George is the yard manager. It was his namesake, George Ausden, who founded the business around the beginning of the 20th century.

Left: George Ausden, founder of the company.
Below: Lower High Street - mid 1950s.
Bottom: The premises and an early form of transport. The picture dates from 1913.

As a teenager, he was a young man trying his hand in the hurly burly trade of dealing in scrap metal. He had already had a go at the greengrocery trade, so he was not one to let the grass grow under his feet. George set up shop at 49 Fearnley Street, with a yard at Stones Alley, Market Place. He dealt in metals, rags, bones, bottles and rabbit skins. George's wife, Annie, ran the business with him until their sons, William and Stanley, were old enough to join their father.

Starting with a hand barrow, George built up the business. He bought two horses, Kit and Black Bob. After the First World War two US trucks, a Federal and a Barford, were purchased. Around this time, after brief stays at two other yards, George moved his base to Queens Road. However, it was the move to the present site and the outbreak of the second world war that saw Ausden's trade grow tremendously. All grades of scrap were needed for the war effort. There were major drives in every town to raise money and reclaim metal for the building of more planes and ships. Just think, perhaps one of the Spitfires flying overhead was built from saucepans and iron railings that Ausden's had collected. One major contract for the company during this war was the demolition and removal of scrap from the Chancery Lane silver vaults. Not only was George Ausden a metal merchant and greengrocer, but he was the local bookie, and raced and trained trotting ponies at the nearby Radlett Road track, which he also ran as a greyhound racing venue.

Geo Ausden Ltd, with its lorries, cable strippers, forklifts, weighbridge, balers and other equipment, is far removed from those times of the barrow being pushed around the Watford streets. The steelstock and container work has expanded greatly and it now supplies the building trade both locally and further afield. Recycling has become a large environmental issue and Ausden's plays its part in addressing the issue, dealing with materials in a safe and responsible way. It also takes seriously its respected place in the local community, supporting charities and schools. Its friendly face is not just for the customer but for the locality both now and well into the 21st century.

Above: Stockyard, Lower High Street, Watford in the late 1960s.
Below: Left to right: John Ausden, Steve Ausden, Grant Ausden, Pete Ausden in a picture from 1995.

Bagging a leading role in the market

Have you got your book bags, children?' 'Yes, miss.' That same question and answer routine is replayed in every primary school classroom at going home time, each day of the school week. There is a good chance that the book bag will be one that has been manufactured by Mapac. It was in 1992 that this company entered the UK education market and began supplying printed book carriers to the nation's primary schools. However, this is only one line of over 100 that Mapac produces. It has a comprehensive range of products in its field, serving a variety of needs in its 16,000 customers. With an eye to the future, Mapac is looking to expand its markets in this country and to build a healthy worldwide export trade. It already distributes to 16 other countries, but hopes are high that this will be doubled in the very near future. The company has already received recognition from the Herts Chamber of Commerce by being named New Exporter of the Year for 1998.

It was as the supplier of polythene bags to the retail food trade that Mark Anthony launched Mark Anthony and Sons Ltd. He had been a sales director with a jute and hessian sack company. It was in a similar environment that he began his company, although it was polythene, not sacking, that was to provide the basis for his success. There followed Mark Anthony Engineering Ltd and Mapac Group Ltd. Mr Anthony ran the polythene company until 1963. The engineering business was sold in 1970. It was the manufacture of the polythene bags at the original company site at Chalk Hill, Bushey arches, where it stayed for the first eight years, that provided the basis for the variety that the company offers to-day. As the company grew, it moved to Colonial Way, before settling at its present address on Sandown Road.

Above left: *Mark Anthony, founder of the company.*
Above right: *The company's best selling product - the book carrier.*
Below: *An exhibition stand from the 1960s.*

are now over 60 people employed in the business of achieving success through a mixture of hard work and innovative thought. Development during the second half of the 20th century has seen Mapac move from the extrusion and conversion of polythene, the manufacture of fresh food packaging equipment and the distribution of Goodyear PVC packaging films into the wider world of sales and distribution in screen printing, school bag design, art portfolios, carrier bags and garment covers. These are now manufactured for Mapac in Europe and the Far East, as well as at home in the UK. Mapac has held the UK agency for the Italian manufacturer Eurobags since 1972, helping to maintain its position as one of the country's leading bag suppliers.

Dennis Anthony has been with Mapac since 1967 and he is the one who has been the inspiration behind the development of the current activities. He has overseen the growth of the carrier bag business since 1970 and was responsible for the side of the company that dealt in promotional gifts until the late 1980s. More recent moves have seen the education venture emerge and, towards the end of the 1990s, involvement in the field of art and music. In 1997, a designer portfolio was launched and caught the imagination of the art retail world. Along with art sleeves and music bags, Mapac has made considerable inroads into a previously underdeveloped market.

Despite hiccups caused by the recession, changing markets and methods of distribution, Mapac has continued to flourish, thanks to the good quality of its products and their originality of design. There

Above left: *The company's current premises.*
Top: *Mark Anthony & Sons Limited.*
Below: *Dennis Anthony.*

Blowing a trumpet for the timber trade

Working with God's own material, natural timber, is a delight that we have all experienced at one time or another. Some of us more than others. Whether it was just in the woodwork class at school when we made our first little ink stand or putting up a fence in the garden of our first home, working with the grain is a satisfying experience. There is something immensely satisfying about sawing and planing that keeps us in touch with the days of woodcraft when man built his home from a mixture of wood and mud, fixed wooden handles to his tools and chopped up logs for his fire. At Brent Timber & Fencing Company you can get a range of softwoods and hardwoods to keep you happy for years on end. Garden decking for that outdoor area makes the barbecue evening with friends that more special an occasion. There is garden and patio furniture to go along with it. Rustic benches and ornamental tubs look so much more attractive than their plastic or metal counterparts. Roses and wisteria climbing through the wooden trellising add so much to the peaceful atmosphere of an English summer's evening. Brent Timber makes sure that you get the best, for that is all it supplies. Treated with preservatives, you can be sure that the planking and timbers

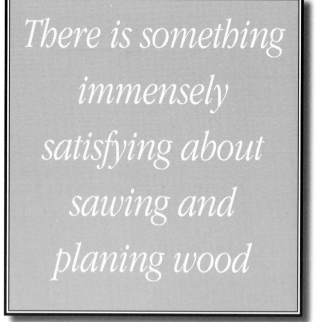

There is something immensely satisfying about sawing and planing wood

bought from here have a long life. Other joinery needs are catered for, from the simple piece of four by two to the grade one railway sleeper you might need for more complex tasks. Look down to the end of the garden at the shed and wonder how it could have been built without the materials and advice you got from Brent's.

The business, sited at the Brent sidings in Cricklewood, was begun in 1921 and officially registered by its founder, John Chapman, in 1929. The yard was leased from the Midland Railway Company. John Chapman was a forester and fencer who specialised in hardwoods. It was not the easiest of times to launch a firm; the days of the depression, after World War I, were hard enough. He worked with a vigour that saw him felling trees himself, with which he made posts and other fencing materials. Other than having support from his wife, it was a real one man band. In the early 1930s Mr Chapman extended his trade by dealing in materials for the building industry. It was a time when house building was fast growing, as the

Below: *The Hosier and Dickinson (Watford) Band in 1927.*

Government tried to fulfil its promise of building homes fit for heroes of the Great War. In 1959, Mr G Hosier bought the business and expanded it. Brent Timber started to move into more commercial work, supplying sheet boards and heavy building materials. The business side of the firm was run by Mr Hosier's brother-in-law, Douglas Lockerbie, until 1992. His son, Richard Hosier, took over this side and has been in this driving seat ever since.

It was in 1969 that the firm moved to its current site at Bushey. There was an established woodyard there. The site, originally owned by the London to Birmingham Railway was the brick quarry and kiln, the bricks used in nearby railway arches; it has been a timber yard since the turn of the century. Concentrating on selling better quality materials, Brent Timber grew over the next 30 years and hopes to have a second yard in the area before too long. It built a timber treatment plant that, as well as dealing with its own material, handled the treatment of timber for other merchants. They were happy to come to Bushey for this service, knowing that there would be a 24 hour turn around in the job they had asked Brent Timber to do. Seeking always to develop further, the client base is expanding at a rate of 20 per cent per year. Brent Timber is part of the larger Hosier Holdings Group, together with sister company, Hosier & Dickinson (Watford) Ltd Building Contractors, but it is good to see that it is not all just about big business. There is still time to act as

sponsor to the Hosier and Dickinson (Watford) Band. Formerly the Watford Silver Prize Band, amongst other names, it rehearses where Glenn Miller last played and now boasts a tutorial and teaching section. It can surely blow its trumpets for the Hosier family and Brent Timber.

Above: *The company's modern day site at Bushey when it was owned by Henry Winfield.*
Below: *The site today.*

The company that has made an exhibition of itself since the war

If you want to make an exhibition of yourself come to Sindall and Baker. That is meant in the nicest possible way. This is a company that specialises in the design and construction of exhibition stands, conference sets, points of sale, receptions, showrooms and allied display material. It is all the same to this family company that is now into the third generation of its management. There is plenty of experience as well as forward thinking to be tapped here. A simple bookstand in the corner, a point of sale display stand or a hangar size exhibition stand is all the same. You receive the same level of attention to detail, service and quality, whatever the size of the order. The main market for Sindall & Baker Exhibitions Ltd can be said to be any company or group that wants to exhibit. The main customers tend to be drawn from the engineering, computing and food industries. However, this is not an exclusive list. With over half a century of experience, no different sort of client is likely to be a surprise, by now. Though you never know, but the company is most unlikely to be fazed by a new challenge.

As with many things, the end of the war brought change to most of our lives. In 1945 a new dawn was on the horizon. Arthur Sindall had plenty of experience of wartime matters. He had been part of the D-Day Normandy landings of 1944 and, having been invalided out of the army, became an assistant camp commandant in a POW camp. As a child, Arthur had arrived in England from Canada, back in 1914. His family were often keen to remind him that he landed on the very day war with the Kaiser broke out. The blame was put at his door! He started his working life as an insurance clerk, before running an import agency with a relative. In the late

> The company's customers are mainly drawn from the engineering, computing and food industries

Below: An exhibition stand from the 1950s.

least they could listen to ITMA, post a letter and get their washing done conveniently!

It was not all doom and gloom. A workshop in Water Lane was acquired and five painters and a carpenter taken on as exhibition work became the line that the firm would follow, eventually with great success. One of the first breakthroughs was made when the company received a commission to mount an exhibition at Olympia in 1947. All this time, Arthur ran the company and Eileen provided invaluable support in doing the book-keeping, accounts and wages. Despite problems with timber shortages caused by the postwar rationing, gradually the work increased and new premises were found on Brightwell Road. So, in 1953, the Sindalls said goodbye to the cramped world that had been theirs and set off on the new leg of their business journey.

1930s he was working as a rep for a firm of colour printers. As peacetime arrived, after the defeat of Hitler's forces, he could not stand the job that he had in export management. He took the bold decision to go it alone and start his own business. Sindall and Baker had arrived - Baker was his wife's maiden name. The firm became a limited company the following year, 1946. This first business venture was quite a simple affair, particularly when compared with the large turnover and size of the factory and offices premises of to-day. Working from rooms at the back of a radio shop in Queens Road, Arthur and Eileen printed show cards. It was a slow and steady job and the business was to stay in the same road for several years. Sindall and Baker went next to rooms above a stamp dealer and then over a launderette. At

Hard work deserves its own rewards and the landing of a large contract for £30,000, big money in the 50s, from the Danish Agricultural Producers' trading organisation set the company on its way to where it is now. That contract, to handle the design and layout of a large exhibition in the main cities in Britain, gave Sindall and Baker the publicity and opportunity to demonstrate its skills. With Arthur and Eileen's son, Robin, in the company since the early 70s, it has never looked back and is already making plans for further expansion to a new and larger site.

Above left: *A recent stand designed and built in Germany by the company.* ***Top:*** *The company's celebrations for the Queen's Silver Jubilee in 1977.*

Dashing away with a smoothing iron since 1907

When Rumpole of the Bailey or Kavanagh QC gets to his feet in the law courts, don't you just admire the starched white of his collar and the gleam of his cuffs? In real life, it is the same, too. Should you be watching a case at a London court, there is every chance that the lawyers' robes have been laundered and pressed by Watford Launderers and Cleaners Ltd. Think of that, as you lie in your smart hotel in the capital, if you are on a weekend break. As you do, look at the sheets and pillow cases - they have probably been cleaned by the same company. Much of the work it carries out is for the capital's hotels, offering a same day service for individual guests. So, if you need a dress cleaning before you set off to the theatre, give the Watford Launderers and Cleaners a call. They will see that you look as pretty as a picture when you step into the taxi for your night out.

Above: John Albert Ross, the shirt manufacturer from Londonderry who founded the company.
Right: An early delivery van.
Below: The laundry in 1907.

The company was set up as Watford Steam Laundry. John Albert Ross was a shirt manufacturer in Londonderry. Stiff fronted shirts were his speciality. They were sewn together by people living out on the crofts in the Irish countryside. These were humble little dwellings, warmed by peat fires - and the smoke and smell from them dirtied the shirts. It was necessary for John to build a large laundry at the factory to wash the clothes when they came in from the crofts. By 1905, the style of shirts he was making was going out of fashion. Drawing on his experience with the laundry, he was pleased to see an opening advertised 'across the water' with the Watford Steam Laundry. It was based in an old silk mill in the Rookeries and powered by a waterwheel. On coming over to England, he soon found that this way of

working was not very efficient. The company had struggled to keep on going and decided to give up in 1906. Rather than suffering from George Formby's 'Chinese laundry blues', Albert, as he liked to be known, saw his chance. He bought the good will of the firm and, with one hydro extractor, re-opened the company a year later on a site he had bought in Sydney Road. It is still here to-day, although it has been greatly expanded to house modern machinery.

The business soon became a family affair. His wife, Edith Sarah, helped in the running of the laundry. Their son, Robert, saw active service in the first world war. He was one of the first soldiers to be involved in tank warfare. After he was demobbed in 1919 he joined the firm. His wife, Edith, was very active in helping the business to

succeed. She worked tirelessly for almost half a century, right up to her death in 1966. In those early days of development, a lot of the work was taken up with the laundering of domestic linen and clothing, usually for the families and their servants in the large houses. There was also a trade with a number of schools. Harrow, the famous public school, used the company. The horse that pulled the laundry cart was allowed a day off each week, as the school was such a long distance away! The laundry does not follow the same suit. It is in operation every day of the year, except for Christmas Day. Eventually, the newfangled form of horse power came along. A model T Ford was bought and a van body added to it.

There have been four generations of the Ross family involved in the business. Michael, a Spitfire pilot in the second world war, joined in 1946. He became the managing director and, later, chairman. He retired in 1988. Peter Ross, who has been with the company since 1970, is the present MD. It was in the 1960s that the development work on continuous and batch washers took place. Watford Launderers and Cleaners was the first company in the UK to use these. It was around that time that the first hotel contracts were taken on. By the end of the 20th century, the company would have a fleet of 30 lorries and vans serving restaurants, commercial premises and top notch hotels like the Grosvenor, the Lanesborough and the Mandarin Oriental.

Above left: *The offices in the early 1960s.*
Top: *The laundry in the 1930s.*

Getting the brush-off since 1760

When father papered the parlour, you couldn't see Pa for paste. Slapping it here, slapping it there..... Well, he couldn't have been using one of the Sovereign range of brushes. He would not have got into such a mess, otherwise. Sovereign has been supplying a large range of brushes and rollers from its Sydney Road home since 1965, but traditions of the industry date back much further. Sovereign came into being when two long established brush makers merged; the Underwood Brush Company founded in 1870 and its rival, Rigby Battcock, founded in 1760. They were both originally based in East London, but were driven out when the Luftwaffe arrived in the skies in the early 1940s. Rigby went to Stony Stratford and Underwood to Watford. When the companies joined forces as the Sovereign Brush Company, it was decided to keep the operation centre at Watford, as it had a larger workforce.

Even as recently as the middle of the 20th century, there were hundreds of small brush making firms in the country, making a wide range of hand made brushes. Stiff competition from Asia and Eastern Europe, where labour costs were considerably cheaper, meant there had to be more rationalisation and mechanisation in the industry to beat off the challenge. Nowadays, there are few general brush manufacturers left. Specialism is the name of the game, whether it is industrial brooms, toilet brushes or those for the artist. Sovereign used to concentrate on the professional painter, but now supplies a large range of brushes and rollers to retail chains, builders' merchants, local and city authorities, as well as BT and the Ministry of Defence. Some long serving employees still make the old pattern brushes on which the company built its name, but mostly you will find machinery carrying out the manufacturing process. Professional and amateur DIY enthusiasts can be certain that they are using quality equipment.

Above: *A brochure for the company from when Underwood and Rigby Battcock merged.*
Below: *Mr Barr teaches new employee the handling and cleaning machine.*

Quiet moments under the beauty of stained glass

There is something quietly beautiful about a slow moving hearse and funeral cortege following behind. Especially it was so in the days when magnificent horses would draw the carriage along the streets and people would bow their heads in reverence as it passed, whether or not they knew the deceased. It is only right that time should be taken when saying goodbye to a loved one. It is not an occasion to be rushed, but one to be weighed and valued as we recall the happiness the departed had brought to the world that has just been left. This is well understood at Ballard & Longman. Based at two centres, 11 King Street and 190 Harwoods Road, this firm of funeral directors and monumental masons are able to balance the sense of joy in celebrating someone's life with the sorrow of realising that it has just ended. The service provided by this long established family firm is built on professionalism, efficiency and quiet understanding. There is sympathy, tempered with the need to be practical about necessary arrangements. The quality of this service can be measured in the fact that Ballard & Longman have served several generations of local families since 1834.

Even in the sometimes sombre world of the undertaker, there has to be the occasional lighter moment. Old Mr Fred Longman recognised this. He loved to tell the story of the American who was visiting the cemetery and read the inscription on one of the tombstones. It said, 'Here lies an honest man and a solicitor'. The American thought it was offensive to bury them

together! He told that tale during the dedication of the beautiful chapel at the King Street premises in 1957. Mr Longman carved the reredos and chancel screen himself. The other delight is the stained glass in the windows. Nearly all were made by the master glass company, Kempe & Co. Originally part of the old Bushey School, they were bought in memory of Fred's parents and act as a perfect background to private prayer and quiet reflection.

Above: *An early hearse.*
Below: *Walter Longman outside the premises in the early 1900s.*

April 1947 saw people having to deal with the same old problem of serious flooding.

Acknowledgments

Our grateful thanks are extended to Myra Campbell and Margaret Griffin of Watford Central Library for kindly granting permission to reproduce images from Watford Central Library's impressive collection and assisting with our research. Special thanks are also due to Victoria Barlow and Watford Museum for allowing access to local images and granting permission to reproduce them in this book. We are pleased to acknowledge the help given by Bert Davis in supplying local information for the text contained in Memories of Watford.

*Thanks are also due to
Peggy Burns who penned the editorial text and
Andrew Mitchell for his copywriting skills*